CHESS
FOR BEGINNERS

BY
I. A. HOROWITZ

Editor of CHESS REVIEW
and Three-Time U. S. Open Champion

A FIRESIDE BOOK
Published by Simon & Schuster
New York London Toronto Sydney Tokyo Singapore

*Rockefeller Center
1230 Avenue of the Americas
New York, N.Y. 10020*
*FIRESIDE and colophon are registered trademarks
of Simon & Schuster, Inc.*

ISBN 0-671-21184-6
Capitol Publishing Company, Inc., editions printed
in 1950, 1952, 1953, 1957, 1960
*(This Simon and Schuster paperback edition is published by
arrangement with Capitol Publishing Company, Inc.)*

MANUFACTURED IN THE UNITED STATES OF AMERICA
41   43   45   47   49   50   48   46   44   42

Preface

IN THIS BOOK I HAVE TRIED TO APPLY SOME OF THE IDEAS
and convictions acquired from 25 years of playing, teaching
and discussing chess. As one observes the games of average
players, the chief impression gained is that they lack driving
force; they haven't learned to hit hard when tactical possibilities give them their big chance to decide the game or
achieve a sizable advantage. I have therefore emphasized
the tactical aspect more than is customary in elementary
books.

The other point that seems worth stressing is that the
treatment of opening play is based here on *ideas and methods,*
rather than on memorizing this or that variation. If you
have a fair idea of what to achieve in the opening stage, you
can follow a specific variation with real understanding. If,
on the other hand, you are not familiar with the vital general
principles of opening play, you are not likely to profit from
memorizing opening variations.

The diagrams in this book can be a great help to you if
used properly. Do not look at them as merely a substitute
for actual play and study. Each diagram should be set up
on your own chessboard, and the indicated moves carried
out by moving the pieces. It is important to make the moves
yourself and thus get the "feel" of chess-playing. It is also
valuable for you to carry out the moves yourself, seek alter-
natives, check on the annotations and find whether you are in
agreement with them, etc. In this way you will quickly become

familiar with the powers of the pieces and at the same time become adept in mastering the details of chess notation.

There are two subjects which generally give beginners trouble. These are the en passant rule (page 23) and the stalemate rule (page 31). You will find it worthwhile, therefore, to study them with special care. Some readers may prefer to skip these subjects on first reading and come back to them later on.

When you have completed this book, you will be able to play chess with pleasure and some ability. There will be room for improvement—that is true of all players. Plenty of play, plenty of practice—there you have the secret of all chess improvement. Good luck, and may your chess-playing experiences be as happy as mine have been!

I. A. HOROWITZ

New York,
October 1, 1950

Contents

1. Basic Rules

CHESS IS PLAYED ON A BOARD OF 64 SQUARES. ALL THE squares are used in the course of play.

The opponents ("White" and "Black") each have eight Pawns; a King; a Queen; two Bishops; two Knights; and two Rooks. Diagram 1 shows the opening position.

DIAGRAM 1   DIAGRAM 2

The opening position   *The King's move*

Note that the right-hand corner square in White's territory is always a *white* square.

White always moves first.

The King

THE KING CAN MOVE ONE SQUARE IN ANY DIRECTION. THIS IS shown by the crosses in Diagram 2. Now, returning to Diagram 1, note how the King is placed in the center of the back row at the beginning of the game.

Ideally, the King can move to eight different squares.

1

But in chess you cannot move to a square occupied by one of your own men. So that, for example, if five of the King's possible squares are occupied by his own pieces, he has only three feasible moves left.

Capturing hostile pieces is accomplished by displacing them. The King captures pieces which are within his moving range.

DIAGRAM 3

The King can capture the Bishop

DIAGRAM 4

The King has captured the Bishop

For reasons that will become clear later, *the King is the most important piece in chess!*

DIAGRAM 5

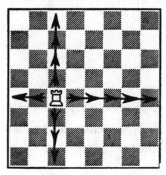

Each arrow indicates a possible Rook move

DIAGRAM 6

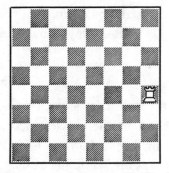

This is one of the possible Rook moves

The Rook

THE ROOK MOVES HORIZONTALLY OR VERTICALLY. IN DIAGRAM 5 the Rook has its maximum 14 possible moves. The Rook cannot displace or leap over any of its own men. It can capture enemy pieces which are within its moving range. The Rook can move in only one direction at a time.

DIAGRAM 7

DIAGRAM 8

The Rook can capture either Pawn

The Rook has captured one of the Pawns

DIAGRAM 9

DIAGRAM 10

Each arrow indicates a possible Bishop move

This is one of the possible Bishop moves

The Bishop

THE BISHOP MOVES ALONG SQUARES OF THE SAME COLOR. EACH player has one Bishop which moves on white squares, and one which moves on black squares. The Bishop can move in only one direction at a time. He cannot displace or leap over any of his own pieces. He can capture any enemy force within his moving range.

DIAGRAM 11

DIAGRAM 12

The Bishop can capture the Rook or the Queen

The Bishop has captured the Queen

The Queen

THE QUEEN, BY FAR THE MOST POWERFUL PIECE ON THE chessboard, has the powers of the Rook AND the Bishop. But, like those pieces, it can move in only one direction at a time.

DIAGRAM 13

DIAGRAM 14

Each arrow indicates a possible Queen move

This is one of the possible Queen moves

In Diagram 13, we see that the Queen ideally has 27 possible moves at its disposal. The Queen cannot displace or leap over any of its own pieces. She can capture any enemy piece within her moving range.

DIAGRAM 15

DIAGRAM 16

The Queen can capture the Rook or the Knight

The Queen has captured the Rook

The Knight

THE KNIGHT'S MOVE IS ALWAYS OF THE SAME LENGTH. SEE Diagram 17.

DIAGRAM 17

DIAGRAM 18

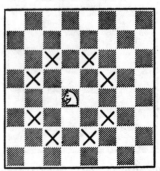

Each cross indicates a possible Knight move

This is one of the possible Knight moves

You can see that the Knight's move is in the form of a capital "L."

The Knight's move has been well described:

(a) one square "North" OR "South"; then two squares "East" OR "West."

(b) one square "East" OR "West"; then two squares "North" OR "South."

Either description can be used to describe the same move! Try it.

DIAGRAM 19

The Knight can leap over any of the Pawns

DIAGRAM 20

The Knight has leaped over the Pawns

DIAGRAM 21

The Knight can capture the Bishop, but he cannot capture the Queen

DIAGRAM 22

The Knight has captured the Bishop, and in doing so has leaped over the Queen

Note that the Knight changes the color of his square each time he moves. Thus, in Diagram 17 he starts out on a black square. But in Diagram 18, having made his move, he ends up on a white square.

Unlike the other pieces, the Knight can leap over his own men and those of the enemy. He can capture enemy pieces only at the end-square of his move.

The Pawn

THE PAWN IS THE ONLY ONE OF THE CHESSMEN THAT DOES not move backward. *The Pawn can only move forward.*

DIAGRAM 23

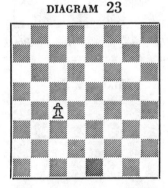

The Pawn, moving from the White side, advances one square

DIAGRAM 24

The Pawn, moving from the White side, has advanced one square

As you have seen from Diagrams 23-24, the Pawn can move forward one square at a time. The same is true of Black Pawns, which, however, move in the *opposite* direction. This is shown in Diagrams 25-26 (page 8).

There is one exception to the rule that the Pawn moves *one* square straight ahead. When the Pawn is making its first move, it has the *option* of advancing one square OR two.

At the beginning of the game (see Diagram 1), the Pawns are all lined up on the second row. (Such horizontal rows of squares are known as *ranks.*) Any Pawn on the second rank, no matter how far the game has progressed, has the choice of advancing one or two squares (Diagrams 27-30).

DIAGRAM 25

The Pawn, moving from the Black side, advances one square

DIAGRAM 26

The Pawn, moving from the Black side, has advanced one square

DIAGRAM 27

The Pawn position in the opening position

DIAGRAM 28

The White Pawn has advanced one square

Still another peculiarity of the Pawn is that it *captures in a different way* from the one in which it moves. It captures one square forward to the right OR left (Diagrams 31-34).

In other words, the Pawn's capture is a limited application of the Bishop's capture (page 4). The Pawn's method of capture, as you will see later on, plays an important role.

DIAGRAM 29

The Black Pawn has advanced two squares

DIAGRAM 30

A second White Pawn has advanced two squares

DIAGRAM 31

White, to move, can capture the Rook or Knight

DIAGRAM 32

White's Pawn has captured the Rook

DIAGRAM 33

Black, to move, can capture the Queen or Bishop

DIAGRAM 34

Black's Pawn has captured the Queen

2. Long Live The King!

Check

THE MOST IMPORTANT FACTOR IN A GAME OF CHESS, FOR reasons that will soon become clear, is the safety of both Kings. When a King is attacked (threatened with capture), he is said to be in check. There are three ways of getting out of check: moving the King; interposition; capturing the attacking piece.

Remember the basic rule of chess: *whenever the King is checked, he must get out of check, if at all possible.*

From this it follows that *the King must never expose himself to check*: he must never make a move which puts him within the capturing range of a hostile piece. *Neither King can ever play to a square which is adjacent to the other King.* Bear this in mind when you study Diagrams 45-48.

The Black Rook is giving check

White's King has moved out of check

DIAGRAM 37

White's Bishop has interposed against the check

DIAGRAM 38

White's Queen has captured the attacking Rook

Special Kinds of Checks

THERE ARE PLAIN CHECKS AND FANCY CHECKS. ONE OF THE fancy kind is the *discovered check*. This happens when a piece moves and thereby opens up an attack by another piece on the hostile King. See Diagrams 39-40.

DIAGRAM 39

By moving his Rook, White can give a discovered check

DIAGRAM 40

By moving the Rook, White gives discovered check

A discovered check can turn into a *double check* if the piece which moves out of the way gives check at the same time. You *must* move the King to get out of such a check.

DIAGRAM 41

One specific Rook move will create a double check

DIAGRAM 42

White has found the Rook move which gives double check

Another important kind of check is the *forking check*. Any piece can give a forking check, but it is generally associated with the Knight.

DIAGRAM 43

The Knight "forks" King and Queen

DIAGRAM 44

The Bishop "forks" King and Rook

In Diagram 43 White loses his Queen, and in Diagram 44 his Rook, *because he must get out of check.*

Checkmate

BY THIS TIME YOU MUST BE WONDERING: WHAT IS THE POINT of the rule which states that the King must get out of check?

The point is this: *if the King is in check and cannot get out of check, the game is lost.* This state of affairs is known as *checkmate.* The King is never actually captured; as long as he cannot escape, the game stops right there. In Diagrams 45-48, we see some of the fundamental checkmates.

(Note that the shorter term *mate* is an acceptable substitute for the more formal *checkmate.*)

DIAGRAM 45

King and Queen administer checkmate

DIAGRAM 46

King and Rook administer checkmate

DIAGRAM 47

The two Bishops administer checkmate

DIAGRAM 48

The Bishop and Knight administer checkmate

Diagrams 45-48 each bear out the same point: one of the Kings is in check; he cannot move to a square which is safe from attack; he cannot interpose to stop the attack; he cannot capture the attacking piece. *It is checkmate: the game is over.* Now you can see why the King is the most important piece in the game, and why he must always escape from check—when escape is possible.

DIAGRAM 49   DIAGRAM 50

White's King is checkmated   *White's King is checkmated*

Study both of the above diagrams carefully to make sure that the White King has no way out. In Diagram 50, note that the White King cannot capture the checking Bishop —for this would put the King in the capturing range of one of the Black Rooks.

Comparative Values

CHECKMATE, AS YOU HAVE JUST SEEN, COMES ABOUT IN THE overwhelming majority of cases by the imposition of superior force. We must therefore know just what it is that constitutes superior force. We must know the *comparative values of the chessmen.*

Without going into the whys and wherefores, you can accept the following table as standard, and reliable for a very large number of all the situations you will meet in your own games.

The Queen	9 points
The Rook	5 points
The Bishop	3 points
The Knight	3 points
The Pawn	1 point

The King is not assigned any numerical value, as his "loss" (checkmate) means the loss of the game.

As Bishop and Knight have the same value, you can safely exchange a Bishop for your opponent's Knight, or a Knight for your opponent's Bishop.

On the other hand, if you give up a Rook (5 points) for the opponent's Knight or Bishop (3 points) you are taking a loss. This is known as "losing the exchange."

If you win the opponent's Rook in return for your own Bishop or Knight, you are said to win the exchange.

However, a Bishop or Knight (3 points) plus two Pawns (2 points), are about equivalent in value to a Rook (5 points).

A Bishop (or Knight) plus three Pawns outweigh a Rook in value (6 points against 5).

If you lose your Queen (9 points) for a Bishop (3 points), you are out of luck. Your opponent's superiority in force will be so great that he will sooner or later enforce checkmate.

When Checkmate is Impossible

AS YOU HAVE SEEN IN DIAGRAM 45, THE QUEEN IS SO POWERful that, aided only by her King, she can enforce checkmate against a lone King. The same is true of a Rook (Diagram 46). It is no accident that these two pieces have the highest ratings in our table of values.

A single Bishop, however, cannot enforce checkmate: the opposing King is bound to have some flight squares.

(Check this by yourself.) It takes two Bishops to force checkmate (Diagram 47).

Bishop and Knight can also force checkmate (Diagram 48).

A single Knight, like a single Bishop, cannot enforce checkmate. Even *two* Knights cannot enforce checkmate! The reasons are complicated, but instances are so rare that demonstration is superfluous.

This creates a dilemma: you may be considerably ahead in material (say a Bishop or Knight) and yet, when you get down to the endgame stage, you may be unable to win.

The laws of chess provide an easy solution to this difficulty!

Pawn Promotion

THE TABLE OF RELATIVE VALUES (PAGE 15) SHOWS US THAT the Pawn has the least value of all the chessmen. Yet it has a power which enormously enhances its worth and affects almost every single game of chess. This is the point:

On reaching the eighth rank (the farthest horizontal row), a Pawn can (in fact, must!) become a Queen, Rook, Bishop or Knight.

DIAGRAM 51

White can promote his Pawn

DIAGRAM 52

The Pawn has become a Queen

Thus you have a choice of transforming the Pawn into one of four different kinds of pieces. Almost invariably, however, the choice is for a Queen—the most powerful force on the chessboard and the surest mating force.

Incidentally, there is nothing in the rules of chess to prevent a player from having two or more Queens at the same time, or three or more Rooks, etc.

The possibility of Pawn promotion opens up new vistas for both players and livens up the game enormously. The Pawn, despite its low mathematical rating, is not to be scorned: its Queening potentialities give it great dynamic power.

DIAGRAM 53

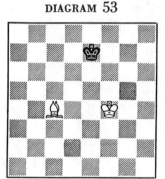

White cannot win

DIAGRAM 54

An easy win for White

In Diagram 54, although White's Bishop cannot force mate, the winning process is quite easy, for Black's lone King cannot stop the Pawn from Queening.

This gives another important application of the table of comparative values. Superior force can be used not only to lead to mate; *it can also be used to bring about the Queening of a Pawn.*

In Diagrams 55-56 Black gets rid of the new Queen, only to find that, as in Diagram 54, White can now force the Queening of his remaining Pawn.

DIAGRAM 55　　　　　　DIAGRAM 56

Black can capture the new Queen
with his Bishop

White in turn will capture the
Bishop

Before we close the subject of promotion, note that a Pawn can only be promoted to a piece of its own color.

3. Two More Important Rules

Castling

WE KNOW NOW THAT THE KING'S SAFETY IS A FACTOR WHICH must be reckoned with at all times. An important measure for assuring the King's safety is the device known as *castling*. This enables you to tuck the King away on an out-of-the-way square and makes it difficult for your opponent to assault the King's hideout.

Castling is the only move in chess in which two pieces are allowed to operate simultaneously. The two pieces involved are the King (of course) and a Rook. (You may recall that *Castle* was the old word for *Rook*.)

Castling with the King's Rook (the Rook nearest the King—see Diagram 1) is called King-side castling. Castling with the Queen's Rook (the Rook nearest the Queen—see Diagram 1) is called Queen-side castling. Here's how it's done:

DIAGRAM 57

Before castling King-side

DIAGRAM 58

After castling King-side

The King is moved two squares to right; then the King's Rook is placed on his immediate left.

Black's castling procedure brings his pieces to the corresponding squares.

DIAGRAM 59

Before castling King-side

DIAGRAM 60

After castling King-side

Queen-side castling is very similar. Bear in mind that there are *three* squares between King and Queen's Rook—and only *two* squares between King and King's Rook.

DIAGRAM 61

Before castling Queen-side

DIAGRAM 62

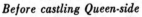

After castling Queen-side

The King is moved two squares to the left; then the Queen's Rook is placed on his immediate right. Again Black castles on the corresponding squares.

DIAGRAM 63

Before castling Queen-side

DIAGRAM 64

After castling Queen-side

There are a number of cases in which castling is *temporarily* impossible:

(a) When your King is in check (Diagram 65).

(b) When castling would land the King on a square within the capturing range of a hostile piece (Diagram 66).

(c) When castling involves the King's moving over a square which is within the capturing range of a hostile piece (Diagram 67).

(d) When a friendly or hostile piece stands between the King and the Rook to be used in castling (Diagram 68).

DIAGRAM 65

White cannot castle, but may be able to do so later

DIAGRAM 66

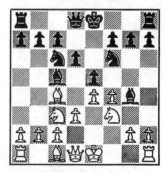

White cannot castle, but may be able to do so later

DIAGRAM 67

DIAGRAM 68

White cannot castle, but may be able to do so later

White cannot castle, but may be able to do so later

There are also cases where castling becomes *permanently* impossible:

(a)   When the King has moved from his original square (Diagram 69).

(b)   When the Rook which is his intended partner in castling has moved from its original square (Diagram 70).

DIAGRAM 69

DIAGRAM 70

White can never castle

White can never castle King-side

A last word on castling: experience has shown that the best rule for the majority of cases is (a) to castle early and (b) on the King-side.

Capturing en Passant

WE HAVE SEEN THAT THE PAWN CAPTURES AHEAD ONE square to the right or left (Diagrams 31-34). There is one exception to this rule, known as capturing en passant (in passing).

Diagram 71 shows the typical setup for a capture in passing. The Pawn to do the capturing is on its fifth rank; the Pawn to be captured is on its second rank and on an adjacent file (a file is a vertical row of squares).

In Diagram 72 the Pawn to be captured in passing has advanced to its fourth rank.

DIAGRAM 71   DIAGRAM 72

Black advances his Pawn two squares

Black has advanced his Pawn two squares.

White now has the privilege of capturing the Black Pawn *as if it had advanced only one square*. If White makes the capture (and he must do it on his very next move or not at all), we get the position of Diagram 73.

Note that this is the same position as we would get from the normal type of capture if made in the position of Diagram 74.

DIAGRAM 73

White has captured the Pawn in passing

DIAGRAM 74

If White captures (normal style), we get Diagram 73

4. How To Record Games

Why Record Games?

EVERY YEAR THE LEADING CHESSMASTERS TAKE PART IN TOURnaments and matches. They produce many fine games which are a boon to the rest of us because of the pleasure and instruction they provide us. To make such participation possible, it is necessary to record the games.

Again, chess books would be limited to the most elementary detail and would make laborious reading if there were not some simple, space-saving method of indicating the moves which are possible or have actually been made in a given situation.

DIAGRAM 75

BLACK

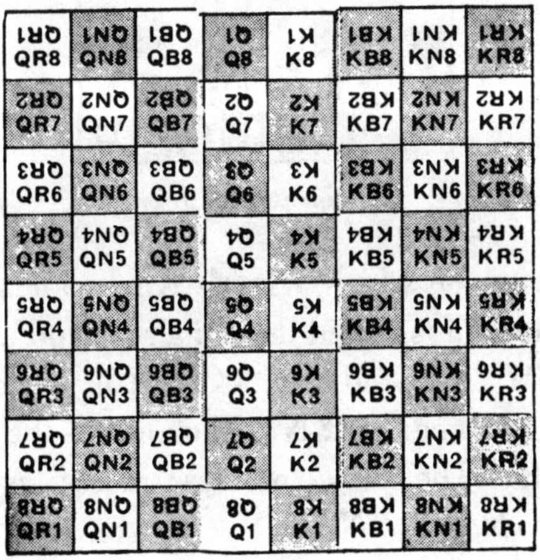
QR1 QN1 QB1 Q1 K1 KB1 KN1 KR1
QR8 QN8 QB8 Q8 K8 KB8 KN8 KR8
QR2 QN2 QB2 Q2 K2 KB2 KN2 KR2
QR7 QN7 QB7 Q7 K7 KB7 KN7 KR7
QR3 QN3 QB3 Q3 K3 KB3 KN3 KR3
QR6 QN6 QB6 Q6 K6 KB6 KN6 KR6
QR4 QN4 QB4 Q4 K4 KB4 KN4 KR4
QR5 QN5 QB5 Q5 K5 KB5 KN5 KR5
QR5 QN5 QB5 Q5 K5 KB5 KN5 KR5
QR4 QN4 QB4 Q4 K4 KB4 KN4 KR4
QR6 QN6 QB6 Q6 K6 KB6 KN6 KR6
QR3 QN3 QB3 Q3 K3 KB3 KN3 KR3
QR7 QN7 QB7 Q7 K7 KB7 KN7 KR7
QR2 QN2 QB2 Q2 K2 KB2 KN2 KR2
QR8 QN8 QB8 Q8 K8 KB8 KN8 KR8
QR1 QN1 QB1 Q1 K1 KB1 KN1 KR1

WHITE

To solve these difficulties, chess notation was invented. A chess notation is based on two elements: the name of a piece which is making a move, and the name of the square to which that piece is moving. Diagram 75 gives us the names of the squares.

Chess Notation

THE IMPORTANT THING TO BE NOTED ABOUT DIAGRAM 75 IS that each square has two names. When White makes a move, the White name of the square is used. When Black makes a move, the same square is given the Black name.

Secondly, the squares get their name from the opening position. We repeat this as Diagram 76:

DIAGRAM 76

The opening position

The square on which White's King stands is K1. The Bishop next to him is called the King's Bishop and his square is called KB1. The adjacent Knight is called the King's Knight, and he stands on KN1. Then comes the King's Rook, placed at KR1. The names of these pieces, as you see, are abbreviated to K, KB, KN, KR.

Going left, we have the Queen on Q1; the Queen's Bishop on QB1; the Queen's Knight on QN1; and the Queen's

Rook on QR1. These are abbreviated to Q, QB, QN and QR.

The pieces always retain the same names, no matter where they move. The squares retain the same names, even after the pieces leave the posts they now have.

The Pawns are named after the pieces in back of them. Thus, reading from left to right the Pawns are Queen's Rook's Pawn, Queen's Knight's Pawn, Queen's Bishop's Pawn, Queen's Pawn, King's Pawn, King's Bishop's Pawn, King's Knight's Pawn, King's Rook's Pawn—or, in abbreviated form: QRP, QNP, QBP, QP, KP, KBP, KNP, KRP. The squares on which they are placed are QR2, QN2, QB2, Q2, K2, KB2, KN2, KR2.

Black's pieces have the same names, and this is also true of his Pawns—except, of course, that their squares are numbered from the Black side.

Let us try two sample games:

WHITE	BLACK
1 P-KB3	P-K4
2 P-KN4??	Q-R5 mate

The final position is shown in Diagram 77. This is known as the Fool's Mate.

DIAGRAM 77

White is checkmated

DIAGRAM 78

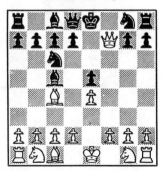

Black is checkmated

	WHITE	BLACK
1	P-K4	P-K4
2	B-QB4	B-QB4
3	Q-KR5	N-QB3??
4	QxBP mate	

The final position is shown in Diagram 78.   This is known as the Scholar's Mate.

As you will have guessed from these gamelets, the symbol "??" indicates a very bad move; the symbol "x" indicates "captures." Here is a full list of the special symbols:

x	captures
O-O	castles King-side
O-O-O	castles Queen-side
-	moves to
!	a good move
!!	a very good move
?	a bad move
??	a very bad move
ch	check
dis ch	discovered check
dbl ch	double check
e.p.	captures in passing

5. Drawn Games

Insufficient Mating Material

IN OUR DISCUSSION OF CHECKMATE, WE NOTED THAT THERE
were cases in which both sides lacked sufficient force to win
the game. Such positions are drawn—indecisive result. There
are other causes of drawn games, as you will see.

Draw by Agreement

A FRIENDLY GAME CAN BE ABANDONED AS A DRAW AT ANY
time, if both players are in accord on this point. The reason may be lack of time to complete the game, or other circumstances which do not permit completion. In tournament
games, it is customary to forbid a draw by agreement before
the thirtieth move. This stipulation is aimed at players who
may find themselves in too peaceful a mood for the kind of
fight that chess requires.

A draw by agreement often comes about through the con-
viction on the part of both players that the game does not
offer either player any serious winning possibilities.

The 50-move Rule

SOME PLAYERS, WHEN THEY HAVE AN ADVANTAGE, LACK THE
skill to turn it to account. In order to prevent them from
dragging out a game unduly, there is a rule that a player can
claim a draw if no capture has been made, and no Pawn
moved, in the last 50 moves. (Note that as a practical proposition, this claim could never be made without an accurate record being kept of the game as it is played.)

Threefold Repetition

THE OFFICIAL RULES OF CHESS ALSO PROVIDE THAT WHEN A
position has been repeated twice, with the same player on the
move, that player can claim a draw *before* making the move
which would reproduce the same position for the third time.
This provision hardly ever applies to other than serious
tournament games. Its application is impossible without the
aid of an accurately kept score of the game.

Perpetual Check

THIS APPLIES TO A STATE OF AFFAIRS WHERE   ONE PLAYER
can keep checking indefinitely, never allowing his opponent
to escape from the series of checks. If the player who has the
perpetual check at his disposal wishes to apply it, the game
can be given up as a draw at once;further play cannot alter
the result.

DIAGRAM 79   DIAGRAM 80

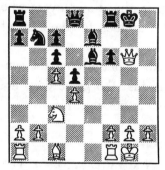

Draw by perpetual check   *Black to move: draw by stalemate*

In Diagram 79 White is giving check. Black has only
one move: 1 . . . K-R1.   Then comes 2 Q-R6ch, forcing
2 . . . K-N1. Now White must make up his mind whether
or not to take the perpetual check.   He is a piece down, and
he has no way of strengthening the attack. So he accepts the

perpetual check: 3 Q-N6ch, K-R1; 4 Q-R6ch etc. Black of course has no choice.

(Note that we write Q-N6ch instead of Q-KN6ch, the "K" in the latter move being superfluous. Likewise we write Q-R6ch instead of Q-KR6ch. Of course if the Queen could go to QN6 OR KN6, or QR6 OR KR6, we would have to specify which square was wanted.)

Stalemate

YOU HAVE SEEN THAT WHEN THE KING IS IN CHECK AND IS limited to moves which would put him within the capturing range of hostile pieces, he is *checkmated* (page 13).

However, when *the King is not in check* and is limited to moves which would put him within the capturing range of hostile pieces, he is *stalemated* and the game is drawn!

In Diagram 80, Black, to move, is in a stalemate position. His King is not in check, but any move would expose him to attack. True, he has other pieces, but they cannot move.

If it were White's turn to move, the position would not be a draw—assuming that White were to make some move that would suspend the stalemate possibility.

At first sight it may seem unfair to you that a player with such a huge lead in material should be "cheated" of victory. But the stalemate is historically grounded in the idea of penalizing a player who is clumsy in making his big advantage tell. The stalemate rule imparts a chivalrous note to the game by making it possible for a hopelessly outnumbered player to snatch a last-minute draw if his opponent is careless.

In recent years, the stalemate rule has been denounced as an anachronism, and the chances are that in the not too far future it will be abolished.

6. The Chessmen In Action

BEFORE WE GO ON TO MORE ADVANCED GROUND, IT WILL BE A good idea to study the individual pieces and get some idea of what each can accomplish. Once we get an insight into the powers and idiosyncrasies of the pieces, we shall be more adroit in making them work together.

The Queen

THE QUEEN, AS WE ALREADY KNOW, IS THE MOST POWERFUL piece on the chessboard. She has the greatest moving and capturing range of any of the chessmen (Diagram 13). She is able, with her King's assistance, to checkmate a lone King (Diagram 45). True, the Rook can also enforce checkmate in this manner, but the process is harder and longer.

DIAGRAM 81

DIAGRAM 82

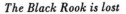

The Black Rook is lost　　　*The White Bishop is lost*

One of the Queen's most feared powers is her ability to give divergent checks; that is, while checking, she attacks other pieces, sometimes at considerable distances. Thus, in

32

Diagram 81, the Black Rook falls prey to a divergent check. In Diagram 82, it is the White Bishop who suffers the same fate.

The Queen also has terrible forking powers. This is shown in Diagram 83, where one of the Black Rooks must go lost.

The Queen is also valuable in attacks against the hostile King. In fact, she is the heart and soul of such an attack. Diagram 84 illustrates such an attack: White begins with 1 P-B6, threatening 2 QxP mate. The only defense is 1 . . . P-N3; but then 2 Q-R6 creates the irresistible threat of 3 Q-N7 mate.

DIAGRAM 83

A Black Rook is lost

DIAGRAM 84

White forces checkmate

Beginners are apt to forget that the Queen's enormous powers are also useful for defense. In studying games which are decided by direct attack, you will frequently observe that the defender's Queen is out of action. This of course gives the attacker a tremendous plus.

Once the inexperienced player is aware of the Queen's enormous powers, he tends to develop the Queen very early in the game. This is generally poor play, because the Queen can then be badgered by pieces of inferior value, whose attack she must flee. Sometimes these early sorties result in material gain, but when they have the drawback of putting the Queen out of play or involving loss of time, the opponent has an opportunity to seize the initiative.

However, such a sortie can readily be entered on when the goal is clear and desirable. For example, if your opponent has badly exposed his King to such an extent that a quick attack has prospects of being successful, then general rules can be tossed overboard and the Queen can be developed early to take advantage of your opponent's mistakes.

The Rook

LIKE THE QUEEN, THE ROOK CAN FORCE CHECKMATE AIDED by its own King (Diagram 46). It is second in strength to the Queen.

At the beginning of the game the Rook is penned in at the corners of the board. As a rule, it gets into action rather slowly, in some openings as early as the sixth move, in some games much later.

DIAGRAM 85

White's Rook on the King file is passive

DIAGRAM 86

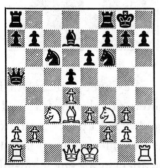

White's Rook on the King's Rook file is active

The Rook needs open lines. As a rule it is blocked by its own Pawns, and as these are captured, the files begin to open for occupation by the Rooks. In Diagram 85 the Rooks

are blocked by their own Pawns. In Diagram 86 a Rook
plays an important role.

One of the most important points about handling the
Rooks is to watch for their utilization *once files are opened
by Pawn captures.* Since the Pawns capture diagonally,
they disappear from their original file when they capture.
In Diagram 86, for example, the White King's Rook has an
open file because the King's Rook's Pawn has captured on
KN3.

(As you can see from the captions to Diagrams 85 and
86, files are named after the pieces which stand on them at
the beginning of the game. Thus, the King file is made up
of the squares K1, K2, K3, K4, K5, K6, K7, K8.)

Another valuable function of the Rook is its role in
castling (Diagrams 57-70). Aside from ensuring the King's
safety, castling also has the additional advantage of getting
the Rook into a more active position.

DIAGRAM 87	DIAGRAM 88

White moves and wins	*Checkmate!*

Once the Rook is on an open file, it often has the objective of occupying the seventh and/or eighth ranks. It
often wreaks havoc in this sector. Take Diagram 87 as an
example. Both Rooks are under attack. 1 R-N8ch would

only draw, as Black has 1 . . . R-N1 in reply. The right way is 1 R-N7! occupying the seventh rank. Now if Black saves his Rook by . . . R-N1, there follows 2 R-R7 mate! On the other hand, if Black's Rook moves along the rank, there follows 2 R-N8ch, mating at once or on the following move, depending on where Black's Rook has moved.

Diagram 88 illustrates one of the Rook's most effective powers: giving mate on the last rank when the hostile King is hemmed in by his own Pawns. (This is a power also possessed, of course, by the Queen.)

Another characteristic power of the Rook, also possessed by the Queen, is the so-called "skewer" attack: the Rook attacks two pieces along the same line; if the first escapes, the second is lost. Thus in Diagram 89, Black's King gets out of check, but then his Queen is lost.

Still another vital activity of the Rook (also of the Queen) is "pinning." This is an attack on a piece which dare not move away because a piece of greater value stands behind it on the same line. See Diagram 90 for an example.

In all these examples, we see again and again that the Rook must have *open lines* on which to function effectively.

DIAGRAM 89

The "skewer": Black loses his Queen

DIAGRAM 90

The pin: White loses his Knight

The Bishop

UNLIKE THE QUEEN OR ROOK, THE BISHOP CANNOT ADMINISTER checkmate when aided by a lone King; the Bishop requires the assistance of a Knight or the other Bishop. Nevertheless there are many ways for the Bishop to assert his powers.

The Bishop, like the Rook, *needs open lines.* As he covers the squares of only one color, it is often catastrophic if many of his own Pawns are placed on that color; for they can cut down his mobility to the vanishing point. Take Diagram 91 as an instance. The Black Bishop on Q3, unhampered by his own Pawns, has plenty of mobility. The Black Bishop (a "bad" Bishop) at QB1 is buried alive. The Black Queen's Bishop Pawn, Queen's Pawn, King's Pawn and King's Bishop's Pawn preempt valuable squares and leave the Bishop very little maneuvering space.

DIAGRAM 91

DIAGRAM 92

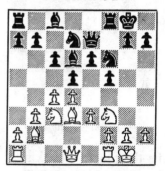

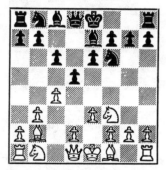

Black has a "good" Bishop and a "bad" Bishop

White's Queen's Bishop is strong on the long diagonal

In such a situation as the one pictured in Diagram 91, Black will be in a bad way if he exchanges off his useful King's Bishop; he will benefit if he can exchange off his well-nigh useless Queen's Bishop.

Bishops are often at their best when developed in *fianchetto style;* that is, when the King's Bishop is played to KN2 or the Queen's Bishop to QN2. This is made possible by advancing the King's Knight's Pawn or Queen's Knight's Pawn one square. Once posted on the "long diagonal" (the diagonal from corner to corner) the Bishop has powerful scope. This is brought out in Diagram 92.

Pinning is the Bishop's strong point. There are innumerable examples of deadly pins. In Diagram 93, for example, White wins the Queen, which cannot get off the fatal diagonal because doing so would bring the Black King within the Bishop's capturing range. To play 1 . . . QxB is hopeless, for then the Pawn retakes and Black has lost his Queen for only a Bishop—a losing transaction.

DIAGRAM 93

Black loses the Queen

DIAGRAM 94

White moves and wins

In Diagram 94 White exploits the pin by attacking the helpless Knight: 1 P-N6! After 1 . . . PxP; 2 PxP the Knight is still attacked and will be lost without compensation.

In some positions where a pin seems well defended, the defender's position can be undermined just as effectively as in Diagram 94. Thus in Diagram 95 White plays 1 P-KB4, B-B3; 2 QxQch, RxQ; 3 BxP pinning the Rook. The situation in Diagram 96 is disastrous for Black; he has lost a Pawn, and, in consequence of the pin, will lose at least the exchange.

DIAGRAM 95   DIAGRAM 96

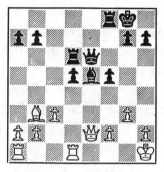 

White moves and wins   *The pin is fatal for Black*

One of the most interesting problems relating to the Bishop is whether this piece is somewhat stronger than the Knight. In master play, the preference is for the Bishop; although he covers squares of only one color, his cruising range is generally much greater than that of the Knight.

While this point is somewhat obscure, it is certain that two Bishops are almost always stronger than two Knights, or even than a Bishop and Knight. With both Bishops on hand, all the 64 squares are under control, and the Knight is at a disadvantage.

The Knight

THE KNIGHT HAS UNUSUAL QUALITIES. AS WE HAVE SEEN (Diagrams 17-22, 43), he can leap over friendly and enemy pieces, and he has the deadly forking power. As compared to the Bishop, he enjoys the advantage of being able (potentially) to command every square of the board. Against this there is the disadvantage that the Knight's move is only a short hop (3 squares).

Note also that two Knights cannot force checkmate, whereas two Bishops can do so.

As has just been pointed out, the Bishop's cruising

range generally gives him the edge over the Knight. This is
particularly true in endgames where there are Pawns on both
sides of the board, and the Pawn position is not blocked. The
Bishop can switch from one side to the other, while the Knight
is rather clumsy and slow in making such changes.

For the time being, let us forget about the Knight's weaknesses and concentrate on his outstanding quality, the forking procedure. In Diagram 97 White has this neat winning
line:

1 Q-Q8ch	K-N2
2 QxNch!	. . . .

Astounding! White gives up his Queen for a mere
Knight!

2	KxQ
3 NxPch	

Now everything becomes clear: by means of the fork,
White wins Black's Queen.

3	K moves
4 NxQ	PxN

Thus White comes out of the complications a Pawn to
the good. Eventually he will be able to promote the extra
Pawn to a Queen and thus win the game.

DIAGRAM 97

White moves and wins

DIAGRAM 98

White moves and wins

The position of Diagram 98 has a deceptively harmless look about it. The important thing to note is that Black's Bishop is protected by his Queen. This is White's point of departure:

           1 N-B3!   . . . .

Attacking the Queen, which must retreat. But where? The Queen can only retreat to a square from which she still guards the Bishop.

           1 . . . .   Q-Q3

The only move. But now comes

           2 N-K4!   . . . .

Forking Bishop and Queen. The unlucky Queen must again retreat, allowing White to capture the Bishop. Thus if 2 . . . Q-Q4; 3 BxB and Black naturally cannot play 3 . . . QxB?? because of 4 NxQ.

In the position of Diagram 99 White has two Pawns for a Bishop and should therefore lose. By means of a very refined series of moves he establishes a winning position.

           1 R-B8ch!!   RxR

If White now plays 2 PxR(Q)ch promoting his Pawn to a Queen, Black simply captures the the new Queen and remains with a Bishop against a single Pawn.

           2 QxPch!!!   . . . .

This type of move is known as a "sacrifice"—White gives up his Queen for a mere Pawn, in the hope of gaining profitable compensation.

           2 . . . .   KxQ

An extraordinary position: Black is momentarily a Queen, Rook and Bishop to the good. If now 3 PxR (Q) then Black replies 3 . . . Q-K8 mate! And yet White has a win in this position!

           3 PxR(N)ch!!   . . . .

By "underpromoting" to a Knight, White gets in a forking check which wins the game.

<pre>
3 . . . .   K moves
4 NxQ   . . . .
</pre>

Now White has a Knight and two Pawns against the Bishop, and must win. This thrilling series of moves will give you a good idea of the surprises and beautiful turns in which chess abounds.

DIAGRAM 99   DIAGRAM 100

White to move and win   *White to move and draw*

In Diagram 100 we have an additional example of the Knight's resourcefulness. Black is a Pawn ahead and ought to win. In addition he has the dreadful threat of . . . N-K6ch forking the White King and Queen. White calmly proceeds with:

<pre>
1 NxP!   . . . .
</pre>

If now 1 . . . . QxN; 2 QxN and material equality has been established. So Black carries out his threat:

<pre>
1 . . . .   N-K6ch
2 K-B2   NxQ
</pre>

With a whole Queen ahead, Black ought to win. But now White reveals his plan:

<pre>
3 N-B8ch!   . . . .
</pre>

White in turn forks King and Queen!

3 . . . .   K moves
4 NxQ   . . . .

Material is even, and the game should be drawn!

A fault frequently seen in the games of beginners is that of playing Knights to the side of the board, where they have little scope. Knights should almost always be played toward the center of the board.

DIAGRAM 101   DIAGRAM 102

 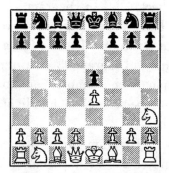

Good development of the Knight   *Bad development of the Knight*

In Diagram 101 White's Knight has *eight* potential squares to which to move (assuming that he is not hindered by his own Pawns). In Diagram 102 White's Knight at KR3 has only *four* potential squares to which to move (assuming that he is not hindered by his own Pawns). If you place a Knight at one of the corner squares, you will find that he has only *two* potential squares to which to move. The moral is plain: *at the beginning of the game, play out your Knights toward the center of the board.*

The Pawn

INEXPERIENCED PLAYERS OFTEN MAKE THE MISTAKE OF DES-pising the Pawn because of its relatively slight numerical value. But even at this early stage we have already seen that the Pawn plays a very important role, chiefly in that its power of promotion decides the fate of most games. But aside from that, the Pawn is often a participant in many of the maneuvers and strategems which give chess its specific character. Thus in Diagram 88 it is the position of the Black Pawns which makes checkmate possible. In Diagram 84 it is the advance of a Pawn which prepares for a quick checkmate by the Queen. Without that Pawn advance there would be no checkmate! In Diagram 91 we see that a Bishop is "good" or "bad" depending on his relationship to the Pawn position. In Diagram 94 it is a Pawn which exploits the pin decisively, and in Diagram 95 a Pawn prepares the winning pinning position. Such examples could be multiplied endlessly, but enough has been said to highlight the importance of the Pawn in chess.

Diagram 86 illustrates another way in which Pawn moves are of importance. White's King's Rook, as we have seen, has an open file on which to operate, as a result of a Pawn capture on White's KN3. The two White King's Knight's Pawns are known as doubled Pawns. In the opening and middle game stage it is generally useful to obtain such doubled Pawns, as this involves open files for one's Rooks.

Almost invariably, when you have a choice of making a capture with one of two Pawns, choose the method of capturing *toward* the center, *not away* from it. Thus, in making the capture which resulted in Diagram 86, White did well to capture with his King's Rook's Pawn, and not with his King's Bishop's Pawn.

The Pawn's "humble" status has some advantages. When it attacks the other pieces, and is duly protected, these others must precipitately flee from the attack. (Obviously it is a

losing proposition to part with a Queen, Rook, Bishop or
Knight for a mere Pawn.) In Diagram 126, for example, the
fact that White's Queen has to run away from the attack of
Black's Queen's Bishop's Pawn makes it possible for Black
to win a piece. In this same diagram, by the way, we have a
good example of the Pawn's ability to trap Bishops on occa-
sion.

<table>
<tr><td align="center">DIAGRAM 103</td><td align="center">DIAGRAM 104</td></tr>
</table>

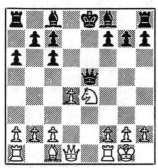

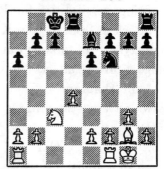

<table>
<tr><td align="center">Black's Queen must retreat</td><td align="center">White's Queen's Pawn is attacked</td></tr>
</table>

In Diagram 103 Black must accept the attack on his
Queen with good grace; there is nothing to do but retreat. If
he tries 1 . . . QxN (1 . . . QxQP??? is of course quite
out of the question, as White's Queen's Pawn is protected by
the White Queen), then 2 R-K1 pins Black's Queen on the
King file. Black would then lose his Queen for Rook and
Knight, which is not quite enough compensation (see the table
of comparative values on page 15).

Since the Pawn is not of much value, it is admirably
suited to defensive tasks which, if performed by a   piece,
would deprive the latter of much of its mobility and power.
In Diagram 104 the simplest way for White to guard his attacked Queen's Pawn is merely to play 1 P-K3: *protecting
a Pawn by a Pawn move is a very economical process.*

Once the King has castled, the Pawns in front of him

play a vital defensive role. On the King-side these Pawns are the King's Rook's Pawn, the King's Knight's Pawn and the King's Bishop's Pawn. Care should be taken not to advance these Pawns as a rule. If they are moved up too far, they often allow hostile pieces to slip by and attack the King. Even if they are advanced slightly, weaknesses are created which can be exploited in a number of ways. For example, your opponent can advance his own Pawns in the hope of creating possibilities for Pawn captures, thus opening lines of attack in front of your King. Or he can "sacrifice" a piece, or maybe two, to sweep away the defensive Pawns and thus stage a furious attack against your more or less helpless King.

In Diagram 105 we have a simple example of how Pawn advances may prove seriously weakening to the King's safety.

1 QxP!   . . . .

An astonishing stroke, but the "sacrifice" is only temporary.

1	PxQ
2 N-B6ch	K-N2
3 NxQ	. . . .

White has won a Pawn.

DIAGRAM 105

White moves and wins a Pawn

DIAGRAM 106

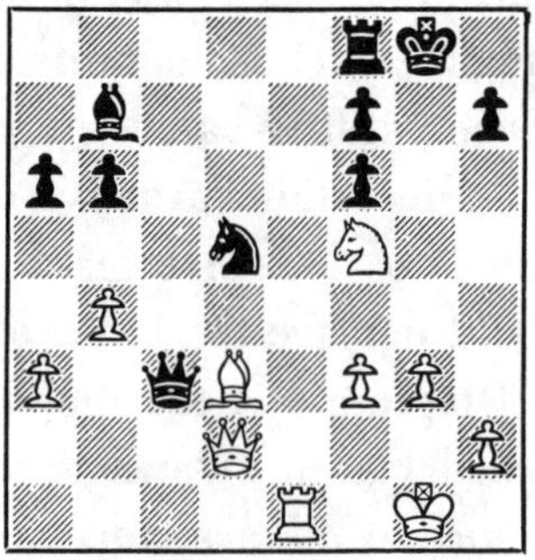

White moves and wins

Diagram 106 presents a much more radical example of a broken-up Pawn position on the King-side. At some earlier point Black has captured on his KB3 with his King's Knight's Pawn. With the disappearance of the latter Pawn, Black's King-side becomes painfully vulnerable.

Look at the position from White's side of the board: with the disappearance of Black's King's Pawn and King's Knight's Pawn, it becomes possible for White to post a Knight very powerfully at KB5 (see Diagram 106); for now the Knight can no longer be dislodged by a Pawn. The Knight is trained on KN7, which we already know is a danger spot for the defense (see Diagram 84). Also due to the disappearance of his King's Knight's Pawn, White has access to the important square KR6 (Black's KR3). So strong is White's position that he can sacrifice a Rook:

1 Q-R6!   . . . .

Threatens 2 Q-N7 mate. Black has no real defense.

1 . . . .   QxRch
2 B-B1   Resigns

Black gives up the fight, for he can stop the mate only by ruinous loss of material.

Another important aspect of the Pawn's powers is its forking attack. This is particularly dangerous for the opponent, again because the Pawn's slight value gives your adversary little compensation in the event of substantial material loss.

In Diagram 107 White is already the exchange ahead. He increases his material advantage by:

1 RxB!   . . . .

Preparing the Pawn fork.

1 . . . .   RxR
2 P-B6ch   . . . .

The Pawn fork.

2 . . . .   K-B2
3 PxR ch   . . . .

Having won a piece by means of the Pawn fork, White is now a whole Rook ahead.

DIAGRAM 107   DIAGRAM 108

White moves and wins   *White moves and wins*

Now turn to Diagram 108.

The winning process is simple but very attractive. White begins with 1 P-K6ch!!—a Pawn fork. If now 1 . . . KxP; 2 N-B5ch wins the Queen. And if 1 . . . QxP; 2 N-N5ch again wins the Queen. An enchanting example of the beauties in which chess abounds.

With this we conclude our study of the individual chessmen and proceed now to see how they work together.

7. How To Spot Combinations And Sacrifices

WE COME NOW TO WHAT IS FOR MOST PLAYERS THE MOST fascinating part of chess: that dealing with direct attack against the King. Such play is sharp, direct, generally decisive, exciting and gives full rein to every player's imagination and creative abilities. When we speak of the inexhaustible beauties of chess, it is generally this department that we have in mind. For thrills and sheer pleasure, it leaves all other aspects of chess far behind.

The word "combination" can be taken to have two meanings. We think of a combination as being a series of moves, at least one of which is a sacrifice, to reach a certain goal. The word "combination" also conveys that the pieces are acting in concert, each participating piece contributing some necessary element to the plan.

The "sacrifice" is the surprise "gimmick" which, as we have already seen (Diagram 99, for example), gives away some material in astonishing fashion, in order to gain something of even greater value later on. The astonishment we feel lends a very pleasant quality to the process; but the success of the scheme gives us a lordly feeling of successful achievement. Of course, when a clever scheme is upset by an even more ingenious rejoinder, our delight is often mixed with chagrin.

Simple Attacks

WE BEGIN WITH SIMPLE SEQUENCES OF MOVES WHICH DO NOT involve sacrifices. In Diagram 109, White wins a piece in a fashion which is obvious and yet not so obvious:

1 NxB!   . . . .

What makes it difficult to realize in advance the strength of this capture is that the position looks quite harmless. Black has not one way of recapturing, but two! Surely he must be quite safe?!

1 . . . .   QxN

This method of recapture turns out to be no good. But if 1 . . . . PxN; 2 RxN! and the Queen's Pawn turns out to be pinned by the Queen: if 2 . . . PxR?; 3 QxQ and Black has lost his Queen.

2 RxN!   . . . .

And now the Queen's Pawn is pinned by White's Bishop on N3: if 2 . . . PxR?; 3 BxQ and again Black loses his Queen.

DIAGRAM 109   DIAGRAM 110

White moves and wins   White moves and wins

Opportunities for divergent checks (forking attacks by the Queen with check) are sometimes overlooked when they require a preliminary move or two. In Diagram 110 play proceeds:

1 NxB	PxN
2 Q-R5ch	. . . .

White gives check and at the same time attacks the Black Bishop at QB4. The Bishop is lost. The important point to remember here is that when the King is uncastled, he is always vulnerable to attacks on the diagonal from KR5 to K8.

For a more complex example of this type of attack, see Diagram 111. Most inexperienced players would not dream of the possibility of a deadly divergent check lurking in this position.

1 NxB	PxN
2 BxN	PxB

Again he must take. But now we have the groundwork laid for a divergent check.

| 3 Q-R5ch | . . . . |

White picks up the wretched Knight at QR4.

<table>
<tr><td>DIAGRAM 111</td><td>DIAGRAM 112</td></tr>
<tr><td>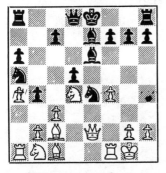</td><td></td></tr>
<tr><td>White moves and wins</td><td>Black moves and wins</td></tr>
</table>

Diagram 112 gives us another example of our old friend the pin—an example so remarkable that it was missed by a very great master.

| 1 . . . . | B-B4!! |

This move wins the exchange. It pins the White Rook

and takes advantage of the fact that White's Knight is pinned by the Black Rook.

Note this interesting point, however: if you place the Black King's King's Rook's Pawn on KR2 instead of KR3, then 1 . . . B-B4!! becomes a blunder. For then 1 . . . B-B4?? is answered by 2 NxB! (a sacrifice!), RxQ; 3 R-K8 mate! (the familiar back-rank mate shown in Diagram 88).

Thus what makes Black's play in Diagram 112 correct is the fact that his King has a "loophole" at KR2. This is a most instructive point which appears in many a game.

Combinations with Sacrifices

HAVING STUDIED SIMPLE ATTACKS, WE NOW COME TO COMBINA-tions which feature sacrifices. Most of these combinations illustrate stock themes which you can study and apply in your own games.

Diagram 113 arose after the following moves:

FRENCH DEFENSE*

Hamburg, 1930

F. D. YATES	V. MARIN
White	Black
1 P-K4	P-K3
2 P-Q4	P-Q4
3 N-QB3	N-KB3
4 B-KN5	B-K2
5 P-K5	N-K5
6 BxB	QxB
7 Q-N4	O-O
8 B-Q3	NxN
9 PxN	P-QB4
10 N-B3	P-B5??

*The opening moves in master games all have standardized sequences with familiar and distinctive names.

Overlooking White's brilliant reply. Now we have the position of Diagram 113.

DIAGRAM 113

White moves and wins

11 BxPch!	Resigns

Had Black continued, play would have proceeded:

11	KxB
12 Q-R5ch	K-N1
13 N-N5	. . . .

Now Black's position is seen to be devoid of hope. If 13 . . . R-K1; 14 Q-R7ch, K-B1; 15 Q-R8 mate. And if 13 . . . QxN; 14 QxQ leaving Black with only Bishop and Knight for Queen and Pawn.

Diagram 114 is a puzzler until you familiarize yourself with the concept of "the passed Pawn." This is a Pawn which has passed the hostile Pawns on the files immediately adjacent. Thus, in Diagram 114, Black's Queen's Pawn is passed, there being no White King's Pawn or Queen's Bishop's Pawn which might possibly capture the Queen's Pawn. Such Pawns are generally very powerful, as they are much nearer to Queening than a Pawn which can still be stopped by enemy Pawns. Dangerous as passed Pawns are, they require the utmost attention to be kept from Queening. There are endless combinative possibilities in such passed Pawns.

Despite the fact that the Pawn position in Diagram 114 seems effectively blockaded, the great master (Nimzovich) playing the Black pieces knows how to engineer a marvelously effective breakthrough.

DIAGRAM 114

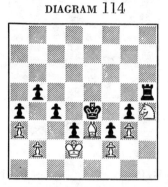

Black moves and wins

1 . . . .   P-N5!!

This looks silly, as White can simply capture.

2 PxP   RxN!!

Another silly-looking move.

3 PxR   P-N6!!

Still silly-looking. True, Black threatens 4 . . . P-N7 (passed Pawn), when the Pawn can no longer be stopped from Queening.   But this is easily prevented.

4 PxP   . . . .

What has Black achieved? He has removed the White Bishop's Pawn, which was guarding White's Bishop. He also has a passed King's Bishop's Pawn. Now the sacrifices continue.

4 . . . .   P-B6ch!!

Now Black's diabolical plan begins to become clear. If 5 KxP, KxB followed by . . . P-B7 and . . . P-B8(Q). For instance, if 6 P-R5 (hoping to make a new Queen too), P-B7; 7 P-R6, P-B8 (Q); 8 P-R7, Q-B3ch wins easily.

5 PxP   . . . .

White has no choice, if he is to keep his Bishop protected. His King is an "overburdened piece."

5 . . . .   P-R6!!

A new passed Pawn! White resigns, as there is no way to prevent 6 . . . P-R7 and 7 . . . P-R8(Q). This delightful combination, which deserves the most careful study, is an impressive example of the power of the passed Pawn.

You have been told that a Bishop can be very powerful in a fianchetto position (Diagram 92) and that a Rook is very active on an open line (Diagram 86). These two points are interestingly fused in the next two examples.

DIAGRAM 115

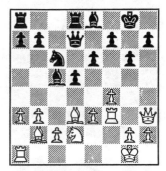

White moves and forces mate

DIAGRAM 116

White moves and forces mate

In Diagram 115 White's King's Rook's Pawn is still at KR2, but White has posted his Queen and King's Rook in such a manner that the King's Rook file has the status of an open file. With the benevolent cooperation of the Bishop on the long diagonal, the following beautiful combination becomes possible:

1 QxPch!!   . . . .

This Queen sacrifice is none the less beautiful for being typical in such positions.

1 . . . .   KxQ

If 1 . . . K-B1; 2 B-B6! (preventing the King's flight) leads to quick mate.

2 R-R3ch   K-N1
3 R-R8 mate

Diagram 116 sets forth the idea in even more electrifying form:

1 Q-R8ch!!   . . . .

A hard move to see—until you connect the combined effect of White's open King's Rook file and his Bishop on the long diagonal.

1 . . . .   BxQ
2 RxB mate

DIAGRAM 117   DIAGRAM 118

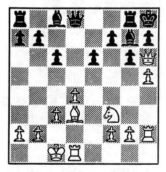

White moves and wins   *Black moves and wins*

In Diagram 117 the combination is based again on an open file and a far-ranging Bishop. But the concluding move has an unusual twist.

1 QxRPch!!   KxQ
2 PxP mate!

The mating move is a double check: check with the Rook at KR2, check with the Pawn at KN6. Black of course

cannot interpose to the *double* check, nor can he play 2 . . .
KxP, as the Pawn is guarded by the White Bishop at Q3.

Mates on the back rank are a favored motif in combination play. But the preliminary moves are not always easy to
find. Take Diagram 118 as an example.

    1 . . . .   B-Q5!!
Pinning the Queen in the manner of Diagram 93. But, as
the Bishop lacks protection, the move looks nonsensical.

    2 QxB   QxB mate!
There is something very pleasing about such combina-
tions. First the sacrifice, which seems absurd. Then the sud-
den realization that it works. Then the final point of the
combination, with its satisfying solution of the problem origi-
nally posed.

Another delightful example of the back-rank mate is
seen in Diagram 119, which begins with a Queen sacrifice:

    1 QxB!!   QxQ
If 1 . . . RxQ (accepting the Queen sacrifice) ; 2 RxR
mate.

    2 R(Q1)xQ!   Resigns
Black has lost a piece. If 2 . . . R(Q1)xR; 3 RxR
mate. If 2 . . . R(K1)xR: 3 RxRch and mate next move.

Now go back to Diagram 119 and try this sequence of
moves:

    1 QxB!!   QxQ
    2 R(K7)xQ??   RxR
    3 RxR   R-K8ch
    4 N-B1   N-K7ch
    5 K-R1   RxN mate!
The reversed back-rank mate is amusing!

DIAGRAM 119   DIAGRAM 120

White moves and wins   *White moves and wins*

And now for the most beautiful back-rank combination of all (Diagram 120). This is taken from a game won by an ordinary amateur from one of the greatest of modern masters (Carlos Torre).

White's Queen is attacked. The refuge is a peculiar one:

         1 Q-KN4!!   . . . .

There is a method in his madness; for if 1 . . . QxQ?; 2 RxRch, RxR; 3 RxR mate. This variation gives us the basic idea of the following play.

         1 . . . .   Q-N4

He must guard the Rook on K1. If 1 . . . Q-Q1; 2 QxR!, QxQ; 3 RxQch and mate follows.

         2 Q-QB4!!   Q-Q2

Clearly either 2 . . . QxQ or 2 . . . RxQ leads to mate by 3 RxRch etc.

         3 Q-B7!!   . . . .

The Queen is really getting to be a nuisance, but she is still safe from capture. And White threatens 4 QxQ himself!

         3 . . . .   Q-N4

It is becoming quite a chore for Black's Queen to continue protecting his consumptive Rooks and at the same time escape the unwelcome attentions of the pesky White Queen.

4 P-QR4!!   QxRP

Forced.

5 R-K4!!   . . . .

You have to have a sense of humor to play moves like that!

5 . . . .   Q-N4

If 5 . . . QxR; 6 RxQ, RxQ; 7 RxR mate. Or 5 . . . RxR; 6 QxRch followed by mate!

6 QxNP!!   Resigns

If 6 . . . QxQ; 7 RxRch followed by mate as usual. As Black cannot play 6 . . . Q-R5 nor 6 . . . Q-Q2 he must give up the protection of his Rook at K1, which is of course fatal. E. Z. Adams of New Orleans was the player who produced this magnificent example of *Cherchez la femme.*

DIAGRAM 121   DIAGRAM 122

White moves and wins   *White moves and wins*

As has been pointed out previously, the Rook can be very powerful on the seventh rank as well. In Diagram 121 White has one Rook on the seventh rank and one on the "artificially" open King's Rook file. Add to this that White's Queen is ready to take an effective role, while Black's pieces are badly placed for defense, and the stage is set for a sacrifice.

1 RxRPch!   . . . .

This Rook sacrifice is made possible by the advantageous position of White's forces.

1	KxR
2 Q-R5ch	K-N1
3 Q-B7ch	. . . .

The Rook on the seventh rank scores an assist on this one.

3	K moves
4 QxNP mate	

The position of Diagram 122 came up in a game played by the author (White) against a strong amateur. The situation is a tricky one, and things are not what they seem. White's Knight is pinned, for if 1 NxR, Black answers 1 . . . QxQ. However, there is more to it than that.

1 NxR!   QxQ

Black must go through with his plan, of course.

2 N-Q6ch   . . . .

The Knight fork wins Black's Queen, but he has provided for that.

2 . . . .   K-N1

Black has reckoned on 3 NxQ, KxR and material remains even. But Black has overlooked the possibility of an *interpolated* check, which has dashed many a clever plan.

3 R-N7ch!!   K-R1

Forced. But now Black's King will end up on QN2 instead of QR2, and this difference costs him a piece!

4 NxQ	KxR
5 N-Q6ch	K moves
6 NxB	Resigns

With a piece ahead, White wins easily.

This delightful example of forking technique concludes the chapter on combinations and sacrifices. We have now seen how the pieces work singly, and how they work as a team. Using our knowledge of combination play, we can now study opening traps (which are mostly a matter of tactical tricks) as an approach to a study of opening play.

8. Traps In The Opening

OPENING PLAY IS CONVENTIONALLY VIEWED AS VERY EASY TO learn. "All I need is to get started; once I get my pieces out, I can play with confidence." Yet the opening difficulties of most players arise from a failure to follow logical general principles which are found in every book and violated in almost every game!

Before learning these general principles, it would be a good idea to examine some typical violations. In that way the later announcement of the general rules will become more meaningful.

The vulnerable King at K1

YOU HAVE SEEN EARLIER (DIAGRAMS 110 AND 111) THAT THE uncastled King at K1 is vulnerable to attacks based on Q-R5ch. (See also Diagrams 77 and 78 for examples of the same theme.) Hence a basic feature of all good opening play is the avoidance of this danger. Two instances of crime and punishment follow:

KING'S GAMBIT

WHITE	BLACK
1 P-K4	P-K4
2 P-KB4	PxP
3 N-KB3	P-KN4
4 B-B4	P-KB3??

See Diagram 123. Black's last move is bad on several counts. First, he opens up the diagonal leading to the potential castling position (Diagram 60). Thus he condemns his King to permanent insecurity. Second, he neglects to bring

DIAGRAM 123

White moves and wins

out his forces, leaving them on their original squares. White has two pieces out (Knight and Bishop), which are ready to get to work. If you think of this in analogous military terms, you will realize that White has forces available for attack; at the moment Black does not have forces available for defense. Play out the remaining moves and you will see what this abstract theory means in concrete terms. Third, the advance of the King's Bishop's Pawn creates a possibility of White's attacking with his Queen at KR5.

It would have been much better, by the way, to play 4 . . . B-N2. This has the positive advantages of bringing out a piece and preparing for castling. It has the additional advantage of not weakening Black's position.

In general, beware of *too many Pawn moves* in the opening. Each time you move a Pawn, you are neglecting to bring out a piece.

5 NxP!   . . . .

A sacrifice on the fifth move, and perfectly sound, too! This tells us at once that there was something radically wrong with Black's last move.

5 . . . .   PxN

With White threatening to smash through by 6 Q-R5ch or 6 N-B7, Black has little choice.

6 Q-R5ch   . . . .

This is the point of the sacrifice. Generally speaking, if a King is unable to castle and is exposed to attack in the center, his days are numbered. This is just about the most basic point of opening play.

6	K-K2
7 Q-B7ch	K-Q3
8 Q-Q5ch	K-K2
9 Q-K5 mate	

With no pieces of his own to help him, Black's King quickly succumbed to the concentrated attack of the two White pieces.

In the following example, the Queen check at KR5 again plays a devastating role.

CARO-KANN DEFENSE

WHITE	BLACK
1 P-K4	P-QB3
2 P-Q4	P-Q4
3 B-Q3	. . . .

As you will discover later on, it is generally better to play out at least one Knight before Bishops. According to theory, 3 N-QB3 would be the proper move.

3 . . . .   N-B3?

While Black deserves credit for trying to develop his pieces, his timing is bad. The right way was 3 . . . PxP; 4 BxP, N-B3. Then the development of the Knight is made with gain of time, as the Bishop is attacked. This bears out the point made above about not developing Bishops prematurely.

4 P-K5!   . . . .

A strong move, driving away the Knight   (obviously

Black cannot afford to lose his Knight for a mere Pawn).
This explains why Black's third move was bad. Note that the
strong Pawn advance would have been impossible if Black
had been wise enough to play 3 . . . PxP, liquidating
White's King's Pawn.

4 . . . .   KN-Q2

(It is the Knight on KB3 that goes to Q2.)

5 P-K6!   . . . .

This Pawn sacrifice should be declined. The correct
reply is 5 . . . N-B3; 6 PxPch, KxP etc. In that case Black
loses the castling privilege (Diagram 69), but he is still alive
—which is more than can be said for him after his next
move. Check your position at this point with Diagram 124.

DIAGRAM 124

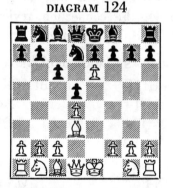

Black's best move is . . . ?

5 . . . .   PxP??
6 Q-R5ch   P-KN3

Now White can play 7 BxPch, PxB; 8 QxR with the exchange to the good. (Count up the captured pieces to verify
this.) But White has better.

7 QxNPch!!   . . . .

A Queen sacrifice—which we know by now, spells
trouble for the opponent.

7 . . . . .   PxQ
8 BxP mate!

The drastic punishment for Black's faulty play is as beautiful as it is logical. The Queen sacrifice involved is of course more striking than 7 BxPch, PxB; 8 QxP mate.

An important moral to be drawn from this little game is that it is very useful to have a Knight at KB3, for then hostile pieces cannot approach too near the King. For example, Q-KR5 is prevented.

Attack Against KR7

IN THESE TWO EXAMPLES WE HAVE SEEN HOW DANGEROUS IT can be to allow the hostile Queen to deliver a formidable check at KR5. But even after castling, that possibility remains a dangerous one. (In this connection, review the play from Diagram 113.) Take this instance:

QUEEN'S GAMBIT DECLINED*

WHITE	BLACK
1 P-Q4	P-Q4
2 P-QB4	P-QB3
3 N-KB3	N-B3
4 P-K3	P-K3
5 N-B3	QN-Q2
6 B-Q3	B-Q3
7 O-O	O-O

Here the opening play has been on a much higher plane than in the two preceding examples. Both players have brought out their pieces systematically (Knights before Bish-

---

* An opening in which material is offered is called a gambit (derived from an Italian word meaning "to trip up"). On page 62 we have an example of the King's Gambit, in which the King's Bishop Pawn is offered (2 P-KB4) and accepted (2 . . . PxP). In the present case the Queen's Bishop Pawn is offered (2 P-QB4) and declined (2 . . . P-QB3).

ops!); less than half the moves have been Pawn moves; both Kings have been castled into safety.

8 P-K4! ....

This move has a twofold significance. By pushing up the Pawn one square, he opens up the diagonal of his Queen's Bishop (verify this on Diagram 125), thus preparing the development of that piece; in addition, the advance of the Pawn creates the possibility of Pawn captures in the center, *with a resulting open file*: White will secure a half-open file for his Rooks either on the King file or on the Queen Bishop file, depending on whether Black's Queen's Pawn captures White's King's Pawn or Queen's Bishop's Pawn.

8 .... PxKP
9 NxP NxN
10 BxN P-K4?

See Diagram 125. Having observed that White now has a clear diagonal for his Queen's Bishop, and a half-open King file, Black wants to follow suit with his own King Pawn. However, he has neglected a simple tactical finesse.

DIAGRAM 125

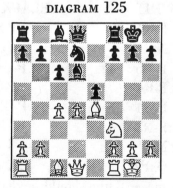

Black has blundered

11 PxP NxP
12 NxN BxN

13 BxPch!   . . . .

This is what Black overlooked. Note that if 13 Q-R5, forking Black's King's Rook's Pawn and Bishop, Black saves everything with 13 . . . P-KB4.

13 . . . .   KxB

14 Q-R5ch   . . . .

A divergent check (forking attack with check). As Black must get out of check, he cannot save his attacked Bishop.

14 . . . .   K-N1

15 QxB   . . . .

White has come out of the scrap with a Pawn to the good, thus punishing Black's oversight.

Trapping Bishops

ANOTHER KIND OF TACTICAL MISHAP IS ALLOWING ONE'S BISHop to be trapped in a net of Pawns. Opportunities for this arise fairly often in the games of inexperienced players. Here is an example with a beard so long that it is known as the Noah's Ark Trap:

RUY LOPEZ

WHITE	BLACK
1 P-K4	P-K4
2 N-KB3	N-QB3
3 B-N5	P-QR3
4 B-R4	P-Q3
5 P-Q4	P-QN4
6 B-N3	NxP
7 NxN	PxN
8 QxP??	. . . .

This loses a piece. White should be deterred from making his last move by familiarity with the principle that the Queen ought to remain at home during the initial stage unless she can accomplish something really effective.

The right way was 8 B-Q5, R-N1 and now 9 QxP can be
played safely. After 8 QxP??, however, Black can win a piece.
See Diagram 126.

Before you go on to the following play, try to find
Black's winning method.

DIAGRAM 126

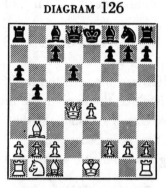

Black moves and wins

8 . . . .   P-QB4!

Now a horrible danger looms up for White: after the
Queen retreats, Black will play . . . P-B5 trapping the un-
fortunate Bishop in broad daylight! Note that Black gains
time for this maneuver by attacking the Queen. However,
White does not surrender spinelessly to the inevitable. He
tries a dramatic counterattack, which is defeated by a neat
finesse.

9 Q-Q5   . . . .

The counterattack: White threatens 10 QxBP mate. Black
could parry the threat and carry out his own threat by 9 . . .
P-B5; but in that event White has 10 QxR, coming out the exchange and a Pawn ahead.

9 . . . .   B-K3!

Black bides his time: he nullifies the mate threat, pro-
tects the menaced Rook, attacks the White Queen and keeps
the threat of . . . P-B5 on ice.

            10 Q-B6ch   . . . .

White is still wriggling!

            10 . . . .   B-Q2!

Still attacking the Queen.

            11 Q-Q5   . . . .

Again threatening mate.   But this is his last gasp.

            11 . . . .   P-B5

Winning the Bishop (12 BxP, PxB; 13 QxQBP) for two Pawns.

Note the difference between the positions after White's ninth move and his eleventh move. In the first case, Black has not yet moved his Queen's Bishop, so that his Queen's Rook is unprotected. In the second case, Black's Queen's Bishop has moved, permitting his Queen to guard his Queen's Rook.

Breaking Out of a Pin

WE HAVE SEEN IN NUMEROUS EXAMPLES HOW POWERFUL THE pin can be (Diagrams 93-96, 109, 118). But there are pins and pins, despite Reinfeld's dictum that "the pin is mightier than the sword." When the King stands behind the pinned piece, the pin is powerful. The pinned piece cannot possibly move away, as this would expose the King to check.

When a piece other than the King stands behind the pinned piece, there is always the theoretical possibility that the pinned piece can violently break out of pin. These occasions are rare, but they have to be watched for. Here is an instance:

QUEEN'S GAMBIT DECLINED

WHITE	BLACK
1 P-Q4	P-Q4
2 P-QB4	P-K3
3 N-QB3	N-KB3
4 B-N5	QN-Q2
5 PxP	PxP

Black's King's Knight is pinned by White Queen's Bishop: if the Black Knight moves away, the Queen goes lost for a mere Bishop. As White does not dream that the King's Knight can move, he plays:

6 NxP??   . . . .

See Diagram 127. White should have considered his last move carefully, if only because of the general rule that a piece should not be moved twice in the opening without good reason. Winning a Pawn may have seemed a good reason, but he soon finds he has fallen into a diabolical trap.

DIAGRAM 127

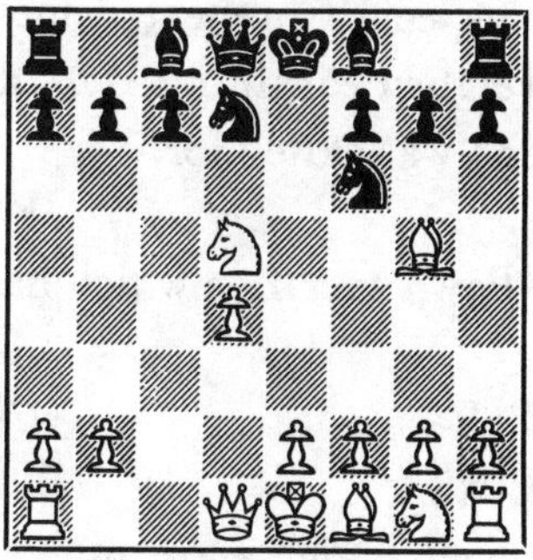

Black moves and wins

6 . . . .   NxN!!

Putting a forceful end to the pin. The sacrifice of his Queen pays off very quickly.

7 BxQ   . . . .

White, as the annotators love to say, has to bite into the sour apple.

7 . . . .   B-N5ch!

The point of the sacrifice. White is compelled to give up his Queen as well!!

8 Q-Q2   BxQch
9 KxB   KxB

Believe it or not, Black has won a piece!

In the next example of this theme Black's release of the pin comes as an even greater shock, for the piece behind the pinned piece is none other than the King!

NIMZOINDIAN DEFENSE*

WHITE	BLACK
1 P-Q4	N-KB3
2 P-QB4	P-K3
3 N-QB3	B-N5
4 Q-N3	N-B3
5 P-K3	P-Q4
6 P-B5	. . . .

Pawn moves, especially repeated moves with the same Pawn, should be weighed carefully. Here the development of a new piece (6 N-B3) was called for.

6	P-K4!

A temporary Pawn sacrifice which had to be calculated with great care.

7 PxP	N-K5
8 B-N5	. . . .

Now both Queen's Knights are pinned. White is following an ingenious plan which has a fatal flaw.

8	NxQBP!!

Calmly ignoring White's threat of 9 QxB.

9 QxB??	. . . .

See Diagram 128. White relies on the pin, as Black's Knight on QB3 dare not move.

9	N-Q6ch!!

A forking check which White has overlooked. As White's King and Queen are attacked, he must capture the Knight. But in doing so, he relinquishes the pin.

10 BxN	NxQ

* The Nimzoindian Defense is a defense named after the great master Nimzovich.

And wins. Black has a Queen for a mere Bishop and Knight.

DIAGRAM 128

Black moves and wins

Unexpected Replies

THERE ARE SOME POSITIONS WHICH ALMOST REQUIRE A SIGN reading "Hands off!" We see that material can be captured. The capture looks playable, and even plausible. And yet the material to be captured is nothing but bait. The consequences of the capture are very likely to be, and frequently are, disas-

DIAGRAM 129

Is 1 . . . NxP playable?

trous. Diagram 129 is a case in point: Black attacks the King's Pawn three times and it is defended only twice. Ordinarily the capture would be feasible, but in this case there is more than mere arithmetic involved. Here is what happens:

1	. . . .	NxP??
2	NxN	QxN
3	R-K3!	. . . .

Sacrificing the Queen for a back-rank mate. If Black plays 3 . . . QxR he is hopelessly behind in material.

3	. . . .	QxQ
4	RxR mate	

In the next example we see Black grab not once but twice. His greediness is promptly punished.

RUY LOPEZ

WHITE	BLACK
1 P-K4	P-K4
2 N-KB3	N-QB3
3 B-N5	P-QR3
4 B-R4	P-Q3
5 BxNch	PxB
6 P-Q4	P-B3
7 N-B3	R-N1

Both players are following good systems of development. Black's Queen's Rook takes the open file to discourage the development of White's Queen's Bishop; a move of the Bishop will lose the Queen's Knight's Pawn.

8 Q-Q3	N-K2
9 B-K3	. . . .

White plays out the Bishop despite the ensuing loss of a Pawn.

9	RxP
10 PxP	BPxP
11 NxP!	. . . .

See Diagram 130. Of course Black never dreamed that

the Pawn could be regained in this fashion. Had he fore-
seen this capture and its consequences, he might have avoided 9 . . . RxP.

DIAGRAM 130

Is . . . PxN a good move?

11 . . . .   PxN?

Why not? Black thinks. There is a good reason for
not taking, as White immediately proves.

    12 QxQch   KxQ

    13 O-O-Och!   . . . .

Winning the wandering Rook and ending up the exchange ahead. So we see that 9 . . . RxP (waste of time by
Pawn-grabbing) was best omitted in favor of some useful developing move.

Incidentally, if Black plays 10 . . . QPxP?? (instead
of 10 . . . BPxP) then 11 QxQch, KxQ; 12 O-O-Och wins
a whole Rook instead of a mere exchange.

In a book of this kind it is necessary to stress the value
of the different pieces and the importance of gaining material and not losing. It is at least equally important, however,
to impress on inexperienced players that they cannot win material indiscriminately, without weighing the consequences.

Past experience tells us that snapping too eagerly at
Pawns in the early part of the game is likely to lead to

trouble. The ensuing difficulties might seem trivial to a master; to the tyro they are arduous indeed. Sometimes the punishment can be frighteningly quick and painful. A celebrated instance:

QUEEN'S GAMBIT ACCEPTED

WHITE	BLACK
1 P-Q4	P-Q4
2 P-QB4	PxP
3 P-K3	P-QN4

Black would be better off to go about his development with 3 . . . N-KB3 etc. The protection of the Queen's Bishop's Pawn seems to be ironclad (if 4 BxP??, PxB and White is hopelessly behind in material). But White has ways of undermining Black's Pawn position.

    4 P-QR4!   . . . .

If now 4 . . . PxP White captures first the Queen's Rook's Pawn and then the Queen's Bishop's Pawn, at his leisure.

    4 . . . .   P-QB3

Logical. If 4 . . . P-QR3; 5 PxP and Black's Queen's Rook's Pawn is pinned and unable to recapture.

    5 PxP   PxP??

DIAGRAM 131

White moves and wins

Even now Black could belatedly stave off disaster by leaving the Queen's Bishop's Pawn to its fate. After 5 . . . PxP?? he must lose a piece (see Diagram 131).

6 Q-B3! . . . .

Attacking the Queen's Rook. No matter how he plays, Black must lose the Rook or "only" a Bishop (. . . B-N2) or "only" a Knight (. . . N-QB3). His policy of clinging tenaciously to the gambit Pawn has been decisively refuted.

A check is the most peremptory move on the chessboard. No matter what the opponent may be contemplating, he must drop his plans to dispose of a check. It is therefore customary, and rightly so, to rely on the strength of a check. Just by way of chuckling over an exception to this almost foolproof rule, look at the following:

QUEEN'S GAMBIT DECLINED

WHITE	BLACK
1 P-Q4	P-Q4
2 P-QB4	P-K3
3 N-QB3	N-KB3
4 N-B3	P-B4
5 B-N5	BPxP
6 KNxP	P-K4
7 N/Q4-N5	P-QR3
8 NxP?	. . . .

Instead of safely retreating the attacked Knight (8 N-R3) White plays for an ingenious combination based on a powerful-looking check.

8 . . . . PxN!

Black does not fear the check: he has a refutation.

9 NxNch . . . .

See Diagram 132. This is the position that White has been aiming for. He anticipates 9 . . . PxN; 10 QxQch, Kx Q; 11 BxPch (double attack!), K moves; 12 BxR and White is the exchange and a Pawn ahead. But he is in for a shattering surprise!

DIAGRAM 132

What is Black's best move?

9 . . . .   QxN!!!
10 BxQ   B-N5ch

The joker, of course. White must now lose *his* Queen too. (Note the family resemblance here to the trap pictured in Diagram 127.)

11 Q-Q2   BxQch
12 KxB   PxB

The upshot of White's faulty plan is that he finds himself a piece down!

In these examples we have seen some of the ways in which the opening can be mishandled: premature attacks, moving the same piece or Pawns too many times, excessive Pawn moves, failure to foresee a surprise counter-move, and the like. Now we are ready to explore the positive ideas which good opening play calls for.

9. Pointers On Opening Play

TO THE BEGINNER, OPENING PLAY SEEMS A SIMPLE MATTER. There is very little happening at the beginning; the forces are just starting to come into hostile contact; there is ample time to get set for the enemy's onslaught.

This view is a mistaken one. In the first place, radically bad opening play can meet with an astonishingly quick refutation (see Diagrams 77 and 78; also the examples in Chapter 8).

Secondly, *what is done in the opening will determine the course of the game.* This statement is not 100% true, but it is true to an extent that should make you very careful in considering your opening moves.

Most primers, therefore, try to tell you what to do in the opening. This advice is generally in the form of "Do this, because...." And that "because" is followed by reasons that cannot be understood by a beginner; they presuppose an understanding of the game that can only come from plenty of study and practice.

In this book the advice will be given in a form that can really be followed by a beginner.

Begin with 1 P-K4

IT IS ADVISABLE FOR BEGINNERS TO START THEIR FIRST HUN-dred games or so *by moving the King's Pawn two squares.*

Some other types of opening moves have obvious disadvantages. Thus it is foolish to begin with 1 P-QR4, because Rooks are only developed late in the opening (page 34). For the same reason 1 P-KR4 is a poor move: in addition it would weaken the Pawn position in front of the King after castling (page 45).

1 P-KN3 (to play B-N2) also creates a weakness in front of the subsequently castled King.

1 P-Q4 is just as good as 1 P-K4, but the initial move of the Queen's Pawn generally leads to a type of game for which the beginner is unprepared. To explain this point would lead us too far afield and might result in confusion. So this is one of the statements which you are asked to take on faith.

Let us then assume that you have started with 1 P-K4. You now have an open diagonal for your King's Bishop, which can soon be developed (brought out). But first it is advisable to play out your King's Knight to KB3 (see Diagrams 101-102).

To sum up: your basic moves will be 1 P-K4, then N-KB3, then a Bishop move. Now you are ready for King-side castling, getting your King into safety (Diagrams 57-60). Castling is generally not played at once, but it is well to get the move in some time *during your first ten moves.*

Other basic moves, not quite so important as the four just discussed, are: a move of the Queen's Pawn (giving your Queen's Bishop a chance to come out); a move of the Queen's Knight (generally N-QB3). Now you can start thinking about getting your Queen and one of the Rooks in action. A little later on, you will be able to study some examples of good development.

Avoid Moving the Same Piece or Pawn Twice

BEGINNERS OFTEN MAKE THE MISTAKE OF FALLING IN LOVE with a piece and moving it repeatedly during the opening. By doing this they neglect bringing out the other pieces; *they neglect their development.* By the time the first twelve moves have been made by each side, you should have moved both center Pawns (two moves), brought out your King's Knight and King's Bishop (two moves), castled (one move), played out your Queen's Knight and Queen's Bishop (two moves). Sometimes a Queen move or a Rook move may be substituted for one of the last two moves.

This gives a total of seven moves, allowing a margin of five moves for captures, exchanges, advances and retreats. So if you have made seven basic developing moves in the first twelve, you can be satisfied that you have achieved a satisfactory development, and are well prepared for the coming play.

Obviously, if you keep moving the same piece, or chasing some piece of your opponent's, or make too many Pawn moves, you will fail to make seven basic developing moves in the first twelve.

Develop Knights Before Bishops

YOU HAVE ALREADY SEEN (DIAGRAMS 101-102) THAT THE Knight is best developed toward the center. This allows us to say dogmatically that the proper development of the King's Knight is N-KB3.

It is not so easy to say that a Bishop should be developed to this or that square. Take the King's Bishop. You might want to play this piece to K2, Q3, QB4 or QN5 or even KN2. So we have the rule: *Knights before Bishops.* The Knight's best square being clearly indicated, an early N-KB3 is very much in order.

As to moving the Bishop: B-K2 is generally a defensive or non-commital move. B-Q3 is rare in the kind of openings you will play (1 P-K4). If you play B-Q3 *before* you move the Queen's Pawn, that Pawn cannot advance and consequently the Queen's Bishop cannot come out.

Generally, you will play B-QB4 (bearing down on the diagonal toward KB7, which we know is a weak point in the opponent's game—see Diagrams 78 and 123); or else B-QN5 (after Black's Queen's Knight has come to QB3).

The Queen's Bishop goes most often to K3 or (pinning) to KN5.

Avoid Early Queen Development

PLAYING 1 P-K4 IMMEDIATELY CREATES A DIAGONAL FOR Queen moves. To the beginner such aggressive Queen moves as Q-KN4 or Q-KR5 look very tempting, but the usual consequence is that the Queen is driven away with loss of time.

Take Diagram 133 as an example. After the moves 1 P-K4, P-K4; 2 N-QB3, N-QB3; 3 Q-R5? (premature development of the Queen) Black develops with gain of time by 3 . . . N-B3! White's Queen is attacked and must retreat. Thus Black's King's Knight has developed "free of charge"—he has gained a *tempo*.

DIAGRAM 133   DIAGRAM 134

Black gains time with . . . N-B3   *White gains time with N-Q5*

Diagram 134 arises from the moves 1 P-K4, P-K4; 2 N-KB3, N-QB3; 3 B-N5, B-B4; 4 N-B3, Q-B3? Now White has a powerful reply in 5 N-Q5 attacking the Queen and also threatening 6 NxBPch winning the Black Queen's Rook. Black must retreat 5 . . . Q-Q1 (saving the Queen and guarding his Queen's Bishop's Pawn). He has lost valuable time.

Note that we have here a clash of two different general principles. Black has lost time by prematurely and uselessly moving his Queen. White has at least formally violated the rules of good development by moving his Queen's Knight twice. However, there are some favorable things to be said about the Knight's move: no time was lost, as Black's Queen was attacked; the Knight cannot be attacked and driven back by a Black Pawn; the advanced Knight is protected by a White Pawn; the Knight has a potential threat of NxBPch (so far guarded by the Black Queen).

To sum up, Black's violation of principles was inexcusable; White's violation is actually praiseworthy. Thus you see that the rules are not hard and fast; they are modified by special circumstances. Generally speaking, the more important the piece involved, the more flagrant the violation. The Queen is more important than the Knight; the Queen must flee the Knight's attack. Hence a violation by the Queen is more serious than a violation by a Knight.

Castle Early!

AS HAS ALREADY BEEN POINTED OUT, CASTLING SHOULD TAKE place within the first ten moves. In this way you get the King out of harm's way, and at worst, postpone your opponent's attack against the King. Beginners often lose games right in the opening stage by failing to castle early, thus leaving the King exposed to attack in the center.

Control the Center

EXPERIENCE AND THEORETICAL STUDY HAVE SHOWN THAT the center squares are of the greatest importance. These, from either side of the board, are above all K4, Q4, K5, Q5. Also considered as part of the center are KB6, KB5, KB4, KB3, K6, K3, Q6, Q3, QB6, QB5, QB4, QB3. But this second group of squares is of subordinate importance.

What do we mean by controlling the center? A Pawn at K4 controls the squares KB5 and Q5; any hostile force advancing to those squares *can be captured*. Thus a hostile Bishop or Knight dare not move to those squares, as it can be captured by a mere Pawn.

A Bishop at QB4 controls the center squares Q5 and K6. Hostile pieces of equal value can play to those squares *only if adequately guarded*.

A Knight at KB3 controls Q4 and K5.

When Pawns capture, they should almost always capture *towards* the center, *not away* from it.

A Bishop or Knight posted on Q4 or Q5 or K4 or K5, if adequately guarded, is generally very formidable.

Avoid Excessive Pawn Advances

WHEN PAWNS ARE ON THE SECOND, THIRD AND FOURTH RANKS, they can defend each other very easily. If they advance beyond that, they often require protection by a piece, a menial task for that piece. Pawns should therefore be placed so that they can protect each other.

Sometimes there are good reasons for advancing Pawns beyond the fourth rank. For example: playing P-K5 to drive away a protective hostile Knight from KB3; or advancing the flank Pawns against a castled King in order to open up lines of attack against him. Here Pawn advances serve a very useful purpose. The rule, then, is to avoid Pawn advances beyond the fourth rank unless you see a very good reason for doing so. There may be good reasons in the middle game; there are rarely good reasons in the opening stage.

Black's Opening Policy

AS WHITE HAS THE FIRST MOVE, HE HAS A CERTAIN AMOUNT OF initiative. As a rule his course will be more aggressive than Black's. If White should avoid premature attacks, *Black should be doubly certain not to attack too soon.* Hence it follows that Black's play inevitably has a certain defensive cast. He is more likely to be subject to attack; he has one less move at his disposal than White for carrying out aggressive designs.

Thus, when White begins with 1 P-K4 and Black replies 1 . . . P-K4, White gets the jump on Black with 2 N-KB3, attacking Black's King's Pawn. The solid (defensive) reply is 2 . . . N-QB3, likewise developing a piece; but where White attacked, Black defends.

Other differences are: while White can almost always play P-Q4 early (after 1 P-K4), Black must often restrict himself to the more modest . . . P-Q3; where White generally plays B-QN5 or B-QB4, Black frequently contents himself with . . . B-K2; where White often plays B-KN5, Black will frequently play . . . B-Q2 or . . . B-K3.

Model Opening Play

NOW LET US EXAMINE A MODEL OPENING LINE WHICH exemplifies the rules of good opening play. We begin with openings in which White plays 1 P-K4 and Black replies 1 . . . P-K4.

GIUOCO PIANO

WHITE	BLACK
1 P-K4	P-K4
2 N-KB3	. . . .

Development with a threat (capture of the King's Pawn).

2	N-QB3

Development with defense against the threat.

3 B-B4   . . . .

First a Knight was developed; now it's the Bishop's turn. Note that the Bishop points down to KB7 and also controls important center squares; and that each developed Knight likewise exerts his effect on the center.

3 . . . .   B-B4

See the previous note.

4 N-B3   N-B3

Each player has brought out another piece—both sides are continuing their development irreproachably.

5 P-Q3   P-Q3

The advance of the Queen's Pawn prepares for the development of the Queen's Bishop.

Now White would like to castle, but after 6 O-O, B-KN5 is troublesome. Black then threatens 7 . . . N-Q5 reinforcing the pin on White's King's Knight and threatening in some cases to capture this Knight, leaving White with an ugly doubled Pawn and consequent exposure of his King to attack. Here is an example: 6 O-O, B-KN5; 7 N-QR4, N-Q5; 8 P-B3, NxNch; 9 PxN, B-KR6; 10 R-K1 (see Diagram 135).

DIAGRAM 135

Giuoco Piano: White's King-side is broken up

The King-side structure is broken up, White's King is in for a strong attack. Black can continue with 10 . . . N-R4 followed by . . . Q-R5. In any event, White would be in real trouble. Now return to the position after 5 . . . P-Q3.

 6 P-KR3   . . . .
This move is generally decried in the textbooks; but in the games of average players it has point *if it prevents a disagreeable pin on one's King's Knight,* as discussed in the previous note.

 6 . . . .   P-KR3
Black wants to avoid the pin on *his* King's Knight.

 7 B-K3   . . . .
White hopes that Black will play 7 . . . BxB so that after PxB the King's Bishop file will be available to White's King's Rook after castling.

 7 . . . .   B-N3
Black loses a move in order to permit the exchange on *his* terms: if now 8 BxB, RPxB and Black has an open Queen's Rook file for his Queen's Rook.

 8 0-0   . . . .
One of the important elements of opening play, as has been stressed, is to castle fairly early.

 8 . . . .   B-K3
 9 B-N3   0-0
 10 P-Q4   PxP
 11 NxP   . . . .

(See Diagram 136). The opening may now be said to be over. Each player has advanced both center Pawns, played out both Knights and both Bishops, castled his King into safety.

Each player has made some moves which are not essential from the point of making the best opening moves, yet no

DIAGRAM 136

*Giuoco Piano: the opening stage
is completed*

harm has been done, because the basic requirements have been fulfilled. Now the Queen and Rooks have to be brought into play.

This is a splendid opening variation for beginners. Complications are few, and it is relatively easy to get a good development.

TWO KNIGHTS' DEFENSE

WHITE	BLACK
1 P-K4	P-K4
2 N-KB3	N-QB3
3 B-B4	N-B3

Developing with counterattack against Black's King's Pawn. This ought to be good, but it has the drawback of exposing Black's KB2—his vulnerable point—to attack.

When playing Black, however, you will do well to play 3 . . . B-B4 as in the previous example. Then, if 4 P-Q3 or 4 N-B3 you can continue 4 . . . N-B3, whereupon 5 N-KN5? is comfortably answered by 5 . . . O-O with an easy defense.

On the other hand, the immediate 3 . . . N-B3 generally leads to crises with which an inexperienced player can
hardly hope to contend, successfully.

4 N-N5!?   . . . .

(Again a word of caution: if you are playing White in
this variation, the safest course is 4 P-Q3, which generally
turns into a Giuoco Piano.)

White's last move is difficult to explain to a beginner. It
has the drawback of violating the rule against moving the
same piece twice; but it has the virtue of attacking Black's
vulnerable point KB2.

4 . . . .   P-Q4

He must break up the attack leading to his KB2.

5 PxP   NxP

(5 . . . N-QR4 is generally played here. It will not be
discussed in this book, as the move has many confusing
facets.)

6 NxBP?!   . . . .

This sacrifice (the *Fegatello*, or "Fried Liver") is un-
sound, but it is effective almost invariably against inexperienced players. It definitely comes under the head of premature
attack; it involves the third move of this Knight; it is purely
speculative. The one virtue that the move has is that it creates
complications.

6 . . . .   KxN

7 Q-B3ch   K-K3

The only move to save Black's pinned Knight.

8 N-B3   . . . .

Adding new force to the pin. Black must augment his
defense.

8 . . . .   N(B3)-N5!

See Diagram 137. Black has defended against the pin,

DIAGRAM 137

Two Knights' Defense: Black should win

and also has the forking threat . . . NxPch. The "books" continue 9 Q-K4, P-B3!; 10 P-Q4, K-Q2!; 11 NxN, PxN; 12 BxP, NxB; 13 QxNch, K-B2 and Black should win—although in actual practice the balance is in White's favor, Black usually going wrong somewhere between moves eight and ten.

This entertaining line is given to show you s ·f ·h· complications that can arise when both players uisregard sound principles. The inexperienced player is advised to steer clear of such violations while he is still in the learning stage.

What were the violations in the main? White moved the same piece three times and sacrificed a valuable piece on the basis of a "hunch." Black allowed his King to be exposed to attack in the center—which is permissible if he is very sure of himself and feels that he can escape unscathed. (See page 118 for an amusing example of this difficult variation.)

One of the soundest openings at White's disposal is the Ruy Lopez.

RUY LOPEZ

WHITE	BLACK
1 P-K4	P-K4
2 N-KB3	N-QB3

3 B-N5   ....

This is the sequence which gives the opening its name. Both sides have made moves which are theoretically acceptable as being good developing moves.

3 ....   P-QR3

This involves a sham Pawn sacrifice: if 4 BxN, QPxB; 5 NxP. But then Black recovers the Pawn with the forking moves 5 . . . Q-Q5 or 5 . . . Q-N4. Here the early Queen move is not out of place, as the Queen's sortie has a disorganizing effect on White's game.

4 B-R4   N-B3

5 P-Q3   ....

Here the masters play 5 O-O, but the text, guarding White's King's Pawn, is simpler.

5 ....   P-Q3

6 P-B3   ....

This provides a further retreat for his Bishop, which may be needed later on.

6 ....   B-K2

7 QN-Q2   O-O

8 N-B1   ....

Here is an exception to the general rule against moving the same piece twice. The Knight will end up on K3, where he will exert strong pressure on the center.

8 ....   P-QN4

9 B-B2   P-Q4

Whenever this move is feasible, it has an appreciably freeing effect on Black's position.

10 Q-K2   PxP

11 PxP   B-K3

12 N-K3   B-QB4

The Bishop takes a more aggressive post.

13 O-O   Q-K2

(See Diagram 138.) The position is about even. Both sides have proceeded systematically with their development,

DIAGRAM 138

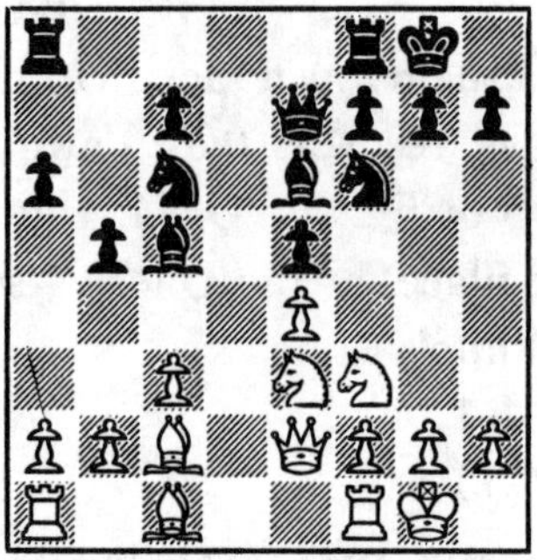

Ruy Lopez: even game

and White still has to bring out his Queen's Bishop. Black on the other hand will have to see to it that the Knight on K3 does not get strongly entrenched on KB5 or Q5.

"Irregular" Defenses

1 . . . P-K4 IS NOT THE ONLY WAY FOR BLACK TO ANSWER 1 P-K4. There are a number of other first moves at Black's disposal. Some of these will now be treated briefly.

FRENCH DEFENSE

WHITE	BLACK
1 P-K4	P-K3
2 P-Q4	. . . .

Having the opportunity to do so, White hastens to form an "ideal center."

2 . . . .   P-Q4

Black likewise strives for a foothold in the center. (Beginners often make the mistake of continuing with weak moves like 2 . . . P-KN3 or 2 . . . P-Q3 or 2 . . . P-QN3, and find later on that there is no room for their pieces in the center.)

3 N-QB3	. . . .

Now White begins to bring out his pieces.

3	N-KB3

Likewise for Black.

4 B-KN5	. . . .

White pins the Black Knight.

4	B-K2

Black unpins.

5 P-K5	KN-Q2
6 BxB	QxB
7 Q-Q2	O-O
8 P-B4	. . . .

When you have a far-advanced Pawn (like White's King's Pawn), it is a good idea to give it additional Pawn support.

8	P-QB4

Black wants to exchange Pawns so that he will have a half-open Queen's Bishop file for his Rooks.

9 N-B3	N-QB3

Both sides continue their development systematically.

10 P-KN3	N-N3
11 P-N3	B-Q2
12 B-N2	. . . .

White has developed his Bishop by the "fianchetto" method (see Diagram 92). Black's Bishop is a "bad" Bishop (hemmed in by his own Pawns, as in Diagram 91).

White's purpose in playing 11 P-N3 was to prevent . . . N-B5, which could be a very annoying move—if permitted.

13	QR-B1

14 O-O   . . . .

(See Diagram 139.) Both players have completed their development now, with the exception of deploying the Rooks.

DIAGRAM 139

French Defense: a difficult position!

This type of game is much more difficult to play than when both players begin with the double advance of the King's Pawn; that is why the latter type of opening is recommended for inexperienced players.

SICILIAN DEFENSE

WHITE	BLACK
1 P-K4	P-QB4
2 N-KB3	N-QB3
3 P-Q4	PxP
4 NxP	N-B3
5 N-QB3	P-Q3
6 B-K2	P-KN3
7 O-O	B-N2
8 B-K3	O-O

Black has "fianchettoed" his King's Bishop, which often has great power on the long diagonal.

9 N-N3   . . . .

At the cost of again moving this Knight, White avoids any possible threats to it on the long diagonal.

9 . . . .   B-K3
10 P-B4   N-QR4

Black is willing to have White exchange (10 NxN, QxN) for then Black's Queen is developed with gain of time.

11 P-B5   B-B5

To retreat (11 . . . B-Q2) is too passive.

12 NxN   BxB

Forced (if 12 . . . QxN??; 13 BxB wins a piece for White).

13 QxB   QxN
14 P-KN4   . . . .

(See Diagram 140.) The position is extremely complicated. White intends a Pawn-storming attack by P-N5 and if possible P-B6. Black's position is very difficult.

DIAGRAM 140

*Sicilian Defense: White has a
strong attack*

The samples of the French Defense and Sicilian Defense should suffice to indicate that the complex type of play to which they lead, is best avoided by the inexperienced player.

Review

TO SUM UP, KEEP THESE OPENING PRINCIPLES IN MIND:

(1) *If playing White, begin with* 1 P-K4. If playing Black, answer 1 P-K4 with 1 . . . P-K4.

(2) *Avoid moving the same piece or Pawn twice,* unless there is some good practical reason for the repetition. You cannot make this a hard and fast rule, but you will have a satisfactory opening if you remember that you must achieve a certain amount of development by the twelfth move or so.

(3) *Develop Knights before Bishops,* especially if the Knight, in moving out, can make an attacking or defensive move. Play the Knights toward the center. You do not have to play out *both* Knights first. As soon as one Knight has been moved, you can start thinking about the best square for a Bishop.

(4) *Avoid aimless early moves with the Queen* which expose her to attack immediately or in a short time. Only the achievement of a definite and favorable objective can justify early Queen moves.

(5) *Castle early* in order to safeguard your King from hostile attack. If you concentrate on development, the opportunity to castle will come automatically. If your development is bad, the chances are that castling will be postponed or become impossible.

(6) *Control the center* or as many squares of it as possible. Here again good development will almost automatically solve the problem. If you move out your center Pawns, play out your Knights toward the center, develop your Bishops on effective squares, you will find that you have a strong grip on the center.

(7) *Avoid excessive Pawn advances* which only weak-

en your Pawns and condemn your more important pieces to
do menial sentry duty guarding exposed Pawns.

(8)   *Black's opening play* must generally be more con-
servative than White's.   Being a move behind,   Black must
generally refrain from premature aggression which may re-
coil on him disastrously.

10. Fundamental Endgame Positions

THE ENDGAME, AS THE WORD INDICATES, IS THE CONCLUDING
stage in which material advantage is generally transformed
into victory. Sometimes the material advantage is not enough
to win, and the game ends in a draw. Sometimes the players
enter this stage with even forces and eventually reach a drawn
outcome. Sometimes they enter this stage with even forces, but
one player manages to win material; or perhaps an oversight
occurs to give one or the other a material advantage.

In short, we generally think of the endgame stage as the
one in which an attempt is made to win by utilizing a material
advantage gained earlier.

How do we know when the endgame stage is reached? As
a rule, a great many of the pieces, particularly the Queen,
have been exchanged. At the beginning of the game, with 16
pieces and 16 Pawns on the board, the position looks very
crowded. Toward the end of the game,with just the Kings,
several Pawns and a handful of pieces on the board, the board
looks "deserted." 90% of endings are with Queens off the
board, and with something like three to 20 chessmen on the
board.

The absence of the Queen gives us a very important cue
for the status of the King in endgame play. With the Queens
out of the way, the danger to the Kings subsides very considerably. Instead of lurking timorously in the background, the
Kings can come out to the center of the board and they play
a decisive role in all endgames. Their agility at this stage of
the game amazes inexperienced players who have been delug-

ed with advice on how to keep the King out of danger in the earlier portions of the game.

King and Pawn Endings

A GLANCE AT DIAGRAMS 141 AND 142 GIVES US SOME IDEA OF how endgame positions come about. In Diagram 141 we have a position in the opening, reached after ten moves or so. White is a Pawn ahead. White's policy is to keep swapping pieces until he gets down to a simple position in which he can exploit the extra Pawn. Let us imagine that he is able to exchange Queens and then other pieces, and reduces the game to the ideal: King and Pawn ending.

Finally he succeeds in transforming his King-side majority of Pawns (four Pawns to three) into a passed King's Pawn. (Regarding the strength of the passed Pawn, see Diagram 114.)

DIAGRAM 141

White has won a Pawn

DIAGRAM 142

Black moves; White wins

Just as the endgame is the stage in which the King is at his most active, so it is also the stage in which the Pawn is at its strongest. The closer we get to the endgame, the more threateningly looms up the possibility that an extra Pawn will become a passed Pawn, and that the passed Pawn will become a Queen. Thus in Diagram 142, with Black to move, we get:

1 . . . .   K-B2

He has no other move.

2 K-Q7   . . . .

And Black can resign. The White King controls the
Queening square, and on the next move White will play 3
P-K8(Q). Then, with a Queen ahead, he will have an easy
time administering checkmate.

On the other hand, suppose it is White's move in the
position of Diagram 142. Then the game is only a draw! For
after 1 K-K6 (all other King moves lose the Pawn), we find
that Black is in a stalemate position! (See Diagram 80.)

DIAGRAM 143

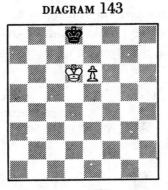

Black moves; White wins

Now turn to a somewhat earlier stage of the same endgame (Diagram 143). The Kings face each other with one
square between them. Whenever the Kings face each other,
with an *odd* number of squares between them, whether vertically, horizontally, or diagonally, the player whose King *does
not have to move* is said to have the opposition.

To have the opposition is often a winning advantage in
the endgame. Thus if White has the opposition in Diagram
143, Black's King has to move. Then after 1 . . . K-K1; 2
P-K7 White wins (see the earlier discussion of Diagram 142).

On the other hand, if Black has the opposition in Diagram 143, he is able to draw the game. Here are some possibilities:

1 P-K7ch	K-K1

We know this is a draw from the discussion of Diagram 142. So we try a different way:

1 K-Q5	K-K2
2 K-K5	K-K1!!

If 2 . . . K-Q1??; 3 K-Q6 and White has the opposition and wins.

3 K-Q6	K-Q1

Black has the opposition and draws.

With the passed Pawn less farther advanced, however, the opposition no longer plays a predominant role. Thus in Diagram 144, if it is White's move, he simply plays 1 P-K6, causing Black to lose the opposition, after which White's Pawn must Queen!

DIAGRAM 144

White wins

Suppose that in Diagram 144, it is Black's move:

1	K-K1

If now 2 P-K6??, K-Q1 and the game is only a draw, as Black has the opposition and cannot be deprived of it.

2 K-K6!	. . . .

White has the opposition. Black's King must give way to one side or the other. For instance:

2	K-Q1
3 K-B7	. . . .

White's King controls the Queening square, and he can now advance his Pawn to K6, K7 and K8, promoting to a Queen and soon enforcing checkmate.

There are times when the opposition makes victory possible even when there is material equality. In Diagram 145, Black moves, losing the opposition, with the following sequel:

DIAGRAM 145

Black moves; White wins

1	K-Q3

1 . . . K-B3 is even worse (why?).

2 K-B5	K-Q4
3 KxP	K-B5
4 K-B4	KxP
5 P-N5	K-R6

Now we have a Queening "race," but White is far ahead.

6 P-N6	P-N5
7 P-N7	P-N6
8 P-N8(Q)	P-N7

See Diagram 146. The ending now arrived at, is not

easy to win, despite the enormous disparity in material. Black
is threatening to Queen his Pawn, but White, by a really dazz-
ling exploitation of the Queen's powers, can force the win.

DIAGRAM 146

White moves and wins

9 Q-N8	K-R7
10 Q-R7ch	K-N6
11 Q-N6ch	K-B7
12 Q-B5ch	K-Q7
13 Q-N4ch	K-B7
14 Q-B4ch	K-Q7
15 Q-N3	K-B8
16 Q-B3ch	K-N8

DIAGRAM 147

White wins

(See Diagram 147.) This is the position that White
wanted to force. With the Black King blocking the Queening
of his Pawn, White has time to bring his own King into the
struggle.

17 K-K3	K-R7
18 Q-B2	K-R8
19 Q-R4ch	K-N8

Repeating the same process.

| 20 K-Q3! | . . . . |

If 20 K-Q2?? Black is stalemated!

| 20 . . . . | K-B8 |
| 21 Q-B2 mate | |

Another way at move 20 was 20 K-K2!, K-B8; 21 Q-Q1
mate.

With very rare exceptions, this type of win cannot be
brought off against an advanced Rook's Pawn or Bishop's
Pawn, as stalemate possibilities turn up. Thus, in Diagram
148, we have a stalemate if it is Black's turn to move. Nor is

DIAGRAM 148

Black draws

White any better off if it is his turn to move; for every time the
Queen relieves the stalemate, Black's King moves with a
threat of Queening. The only way to prevent this is to drive

the King to R8, whereupon the stalemate threat turns up again.
A Rook's Pawn is often involved in other stalemate possibilities. For instance, in Diagram 149, White cannot win
because he can never drive the Black King away from the
Queening square. Even losing the opposition does not affect
the outcome. Suppose Black moves first:

DIAGRAM 149

White can only draw

1	K-N1
2 K-N6	K-R1
3 P-R5	K-N1
4 P-R6	K-R1
5 P-R7	. . . .

Black is of course stalemated. Move all the forces one
file to the left, and White would have an easy win. In this
ending one sees a great disadvantage in having a Rook's
Pawn.

There are times, however, when a Rook's Pawn can be
very strong.

In Diagram 150, White's Pawn is not only a passed Pawn
—it is a "remote passed Pawn." As the term connotes, such a
Pawn is far away from the opposing King who must try to
stop the Pawn from Queening. Here the remote passed Pawn
Queens without the aid of its own King.

DIAGRAM 150

The Pawn wins unaided

1 P-R4	K-N1
2 P-R5	K-B1
3 P-R6	K-K1
4 P-R7	K-B1
5 P-R8(Q)ch	

And White soon forces checkmate.

The remote passed Pawn has many valuable uses. In Diagram 151 material is even, but an expert can see at a glance

DIAGRAM 151

White wins

that White has an easy win. Black's extra Pawn on the Kingside has no significance, while White's Pawn on the other

wing forces Black's King to concentrate his attention on it.
Play proceeds:

1	P-R5	K-Q3
2	K-B5	K-B3

Black cannot stop the coming invasion, as he must keep
his eye on the remote passed Pawn.

3	K-N6	K-N4
4	KxP	KxP
5	KxP	....

And White will soon make a new Queen.

Finally, an amusing stratagem which often turns up in
races to make a new Queen (see Diagram 152):

DIAGRAM 152

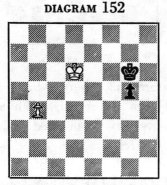

White moves and wins

1	P-N5	P-N5

As he cannot stop the White Pawn, he has no choice but
to try his luck with his own passed Pawn.

2	P-N6	P-N6
3	P-N7	P-N7
4	P-N8(Q)	P-N8(Q)

So far so good. But....

5	Q-N8ch!	....

Winning Black's Queen, and the game!

Rook and Pawn Endings

THESE ARE PERHAPS THE MOST FREQUENT OF ALL TYPES OF endgames. It is of the greatest importance to keep both King and Rook mobile, as fast action and aggressive spirit play an important role. The basic position of Rook and Pawn endings

DIAGRAM 153

White wins

is shown in Diagram 153, where a Pawn is on the seventh rank waiting to Queen. At first sight White's trouble is that his King cannot move. This is remedied by:

1 R-Q1ch   K-B2

If now 2 K-K7, R-K7ch; 3 K-B6, R-B7ch; 4 K-K6, R-K7ch; 5 K-B5, R-B7ch and as White's King has to keep protecting the Pawn, he cannot make any progress.

The winning idea, then, is to maneuver with the White Rook in such a way as to be able to interpose to Black's checks. At the same time, of course, the Black King must be made to keep his distance. Thus, if 2 R-K1 (to enable White's King to go to K7 without being checked), Black replies 2 . . . K-Q2 or . . . K-Q1.

2 R-Q4!   R-N8
3 K-K7   R-K8ch
4 K-B6   R-B8ch

5 K-N6	R-N8ch
6 K-B5	R-B8ch
7 R-KB4!	. . . .

And now White's Pawn can no longer be prevented from Queening. This is a very important ending with which every player should be familiar. Opportunities for playing it occur frequently.

When the extra Pawn is a Rook's Pawn, the weaker side often has good drawing chances. On the other hand, there are times when a distant passed Pawn can participate in an ingenious little stratagem (Diagram 154):

DIAGRAM 154

White moves and wins

1 R-R8!   . . . .

To desert the precious passed Pawn like this comes as a shock. It is the only way to win!

1 . . . .   RxP

Else the Pawn becomes a Queen.

2 R-R7ch   . . . .

And White wins the Rook. This is an example of the "skewer" (Diagram 89).

Other Types of Endings

IT WOULD BE GOING TOO FAR AFIELD IN A BOOK OF THIS SCOPE
to discuss the endgame in detail, but the following comments
should be helpful:

The Bishop is generally superior to the Knight in an
ending, unless the Pawn position is barricaded. Where the
Pawn position is fluid and where there are Pawns on both
wings, the long-range Bishop will generally outplay the short-
stepping Knight.

In endings with a Bishop and some Pawns on each side,
the player with a Pawn ahead will generally make his advantage tell.

In such endings, when material is even, the player who
has a "bad" Bishop (see Diagram 91) will generally lose
the game because of his lack of mobility.

In endings with "Bishops of opposite colors" (one player has a Bishop traveling on white squares, while his opponent
has a Bishop traveling on black squares), the usual result is a
draw, even where one player is a Pawn ahead. This is due to
the likelihood that the player who is behind in material can
adopt a blockade position on the squares which he controls.

One of the most interesting examples of how the outcome

DIAGRAM 155

White wins easily

can be affected by the color of the Bishop's squares is seen
in Diagrams 155-156. In Diagram 155 White wins at once:

1 B-K5ch	K-N1
2 P-R7ch	K-B1
3 P-R8(Q)ch	. . . .

Obviously White has a quick mate. You would think that
the material advantage of a Bishop and Pawn automatically
wins very easily for White; yet the win is only possible in
Diagram 155 because the Queening square is of the same color
as those on which the Bishop travels!

Sounds incredible, doesn't it? But consider Diagram
156: If 1 P-R7, Black is stalemated (see Diagram 80). If 1

DIAGRAM 156

White cannot win!

B-Q5, Black is again stalemated. The Black King remains on
the Queening square, and there is no way to smoke him out!
The trouble is, of course, that the Queening square is a black
square, while White's Bishop travels only on white squares.

The advantage of the exchange generally wins easily for
the player with the Rook. That is to say, in an ending of Rook
and Pawns against Bishop (or Knight) and the same number
of Pawns, the Rook will almost always prove superior because of its greater mobility. The Rook will generally win,
also, when the weaker side has one Pawn for the exchange.

But Bishop (or Knight) and two Pawns against a Rook usually leads to a draw.

Endings of Queens and Pawns are difficult to play because of the Queen's highly developed checking powers. In such endings an advantage in material is often nullified by a perpetual check.

In endings of King and Rook against King and Bishop (or Knight), with no Pawns involved, the weaker side can usually draw. Losing positions come about when the weaker side's King can be forced to one of the ranks at the edge of the board. The resulting mating possibilities may make it possible for the Rook to triumph.

Thus in Diagram 157 White need only make a "tempo-move" to put Black in "Zugzwang."

DIAGRAM 157

White wins quickly

                1 R-QR7   . . . .

This is the tempo-move: White simply marks time. 1 R-Q7 or 1 R-QB7 serves the same purpose.

                1 . . . .   K-B1

Black is in "Zugzwang" (a German word meaning move-compulsion). If 1 . . . N-B2 or 1 . . . N-N3 the Knight is lost. "Zugzwang" is the term applied to situations where loss of material is occasioned by having to move.

   2 R-R8 mate

   A lone Rook usually draws against Rook and Bishop (or Knight) except when the weaker side's King is forced to the edge of the board. In the latter case there are mating possibilities which may prove decisive.

DIAGRAM 158

White wins quickly

   Diagram 158 shows a particularly unfavorable situation for the weaker side:

   1 B-B4!   . . . .

Threatens R-N8 mate and prevents Black's Rook from giving any annoying checks.

1	K-B1
2 B-K6ch	K-Q1
3 R-N8ch	. . . .

And White mates next move.

   In concluding the section on endgame play, a few general principles will be found useful. The endgame is the special domain devoted to exploiting material advantages. The Pawn becomes enormously important here, as its Queening possibilities are magnified. The King at last plays an active role, attacking hostile Pawns, guarding his own, escorting passed Pawns to the Queening square.   Rooks should strive for mobility—posted on the seventh rank, or on open files, or behind their own passed Pawns. Bishops are best on open diagonals; beware of having a bad Bishop which is hemmed in by its own Pawns. If you have a choice, try to retain a Bishop rather than a Knight for the endgame.

In short: material advantage plus mobility spells victory in the endgame. Mobility in materially even positions will often lead to material advantage.   Mobility will often neutralize one's material disadvantage. Mobility is the key to almost all types of endings.

11. Illustrative Games

IN THIS CHAPTER, WE SHALL NOW TRY TO APPLY WHAT WE have learned in the earlier sections of this book about the opening and middle game play. Mistakes are drastically punished here, in order to drive the lessons home; in "real life," the players who blunder often escape scot-free!

GIUOCO PIANO
Berlin, 1907

T. VON SCHEVE	R. TEICHMANN
White	Black
1 P-K4	P-K4
2 N-KB3	N-QB3
3 B-B4	B-B4
4 P-B3	....

White intends to play P-Q4, getting a powerful Pawn center and driving away Black's pieces from that sector.

4	Q-K2

This early Queen move is permissible because it does not expose Black's Queen to attack and because it is part of a plan to maintain Black's hold on the center.

5 O-O	P-Q3
6 P-Q4	B-N3
7 P-QR4	....

The Pawn advance involves a very complicated threat: 8 P-R5, BxRP?; 9 P-Q5, N-N1; 10 RxB and Black has lost a piece for a Pawn. Or 8 P-R5, NxRP; 9 RxN, BxR; 10 Q-R4ch winning the Bishop and coming out with two pieces for Rook and Pawn—material advantage for White.

        7 . . . .   P-QR3

        8 P-R5   B-R2

But here he could play 8 . . . NxRP; 9 RxN, BxR; 10 Q-R4ch, P-QN4; 11 QxB, PxB with the exchange ahead.

        9 P-R3   . . . .

In order to prevent a pin on his King's Knight by . . . B-N5.

        9 . . . .   N-B3

DIAGRAM 159

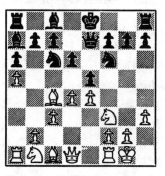

How should White continue?

See Diagram 159. White should now play R-K1, followed by the development of his Queen-side pieces.

        10 PxP?   . . . .

But this is quite pointless. It opens up the diagonal for Black's Bishop at QR2, which is now trained directly on White's King. At the same time the Black Knight on QB3 reaches a more aggressive post at K4.

        10 . . . .   QNxP

        11 NxN   . . . .

Rather than lose time by retreating his attacked Bishop at QB4, White prefers to exchange. But now Black's Queen comes powerfully into play.

11	QxN
12 N-Q2	. . . .

He does not see what is coming!

12	BxRP!

The purpose of this sacrifice is to break up the Pawn position in front of White's King.

13 PxB	Q-N6ch

Second point of the sacrifice: White's King's Bishop's Pawn is pinned (check the note to White's 10th move).

DIAGRAM 160

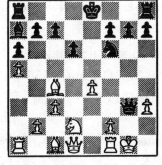

Black's Queen is immune!

14 K-R1	QxRPch
15 K-N1	N-N5

Threatens . . . Q-R7 mate. This is an object lesson in what happens once the Pawn wall in front of the castled King is breached.

16 N-B3	Q-N6ch

The Queen still cannot be captured.

17 K-R1	BxP

White resigns. (See Diagram 161.) Black threatens 18 . . . Q-R6ch; 19 N-R2, QxN mate.

White has nothing better than 18 B-B4, QxB; but then he is three Pawns down and 19 . . . Q-N6 will be deadly.

DIAGRAM 161

White is lost

This simple but very instructive game is worthy of careful study.

TWO KNIGHTS' DEFENSE

New Orleans, 1858

P. MORPHY   AMATEUR
White   Black

(*Remove White's Queen's Rook**)

	P. MORPHY White	AMATEUR Black
1	P-K4	P-K4
2	N-KB3	N-QB3
3	B-B4	N-B3
4	N-N5	P-Q4
5	PxP	NxP

If Black wants to avoid the coming complications, he can play 5 . . . N-QR4. For a discussion of this line of play see page 90.

6 NxBP?!   . . . .

See Diagram 162. With White a Rook down to begin with, his sacrifice shows sublime self-confidence!

* White is giving the odds of his Queen's Rook, *i.e.* he is playing without that piece. Odds-giving was once very popular, the idea being to give the weaker player a fighting chance.

DIAGRAM 162

The "Fried Liver" Attack!

6	KxN
7 Q-B3ch	K-K3
8 N-B3	N-Q5?

Why throw the pinned Knight to the wolves? 8 . . . N(B3)-K2 holds all his booty without any danger.

| 9 BxNch | K-Q3 |
| 10 Q-B7 | . . . . |

White threatens 11 N-K4 mate. See Diagram 163.

DIAGRAM 163

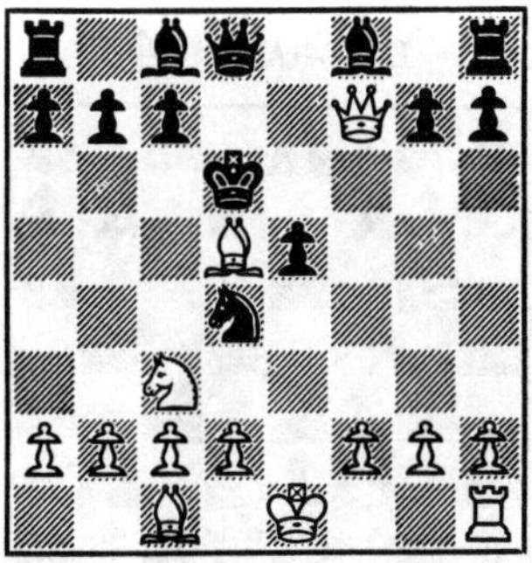

How should Black block the mating threat?

| 10 . . . . | B-K3? |

This stops the mate, but 10 . . . Q-K2! wás a much better method. When you are under attack and are ahead in material, it is generally good policy to offer the exchange of Queens.

11 BxB	NxB
12 N-K4ch	K-Q4
13 P-QB4ch!?	. . . .

Sheer bluff is White's only weapon, and he does not shrink from using it.

13	KxN
14 QxN	Q-Q5?

After 14 . . . K-Q5! White would be hard put to it to accomplish anything, despite the Black King's exposed situation.

15 Q-N4ch	K-Q6
16 Q-K2ch	K-B7
17 P-Q3 dis ch!	KxB

If instead 17 . . . K-N8; 18 O-O, KxP; 19 Q-B2! and White's coming discovered check with the Queen's Knight's Pawn will be deadly.

18 O-O mate !!!

DIAGRAM 164

One of the most beautiful mates ever seen!

See Diagram 164. This beautiful checkmate gives us some idea of the dangers which surround a King who is under attack on the open board. The winner of this game, Paul Morphy, is considered by many the greatest player who ever lived.

FRENCH DEFENSE

Albany, 1950

B. SACKMAN	J. RICARD
White	Black
1 P-K4	P-K3
2 P-Q4	P-Q4

With the Black King's Pawn on K3 and the Queen's Pawn on Q4, Black's Queen's Bishop is a "bad" Bishop and is likely to have little mobility. This hemming in of the Bishop by his own Pawns is one of the drawbacks of the French Defense.

3 PxP	PxP

White's third move (hardly ever adopted in master play) frees Black's Queen's Bishop, which can now be freely developed.

4 N-QB3	N-KB3
5 N-B3	B-KB4

5 . . . B-KN5 (pinning) seems more natural. As Black plays, White's King's Knight later occupies K5 very strongly.

6 B-Q3	BxB
7 QxB	B-Q3
8 O-O	O-O
9 R-K1	. . . .

Both players have developed in normal fashion, and now White plays his Rook to the open file.

9	P-B3
10 N-K5!	. . . .

See Diagram 165. The Knight is strongly posted here. Nor would exchanging help Black: after 10 . . . BxN; 11 PxB, KN-Q2; 12 Q-N3 White has a strong attacking position, chiefly due to the enforced absence of Black's King's Knight from his best defensive square (KB3).

DIAGRAM 165

White's Knight at K5 is powerfully posted

10	Q-B2
11 Q-N3	. . . .

Now Black is in a quandary, as the powerful pinning move 12 B-R6 (mating threat!) is contemplated by White.

| 11 . . . . | N-K5? |

Black attempts to create a diversion by what he thinks is a pseudo-sacrifice.

| 12 NxN | PxN |

Here is what Black is getting at: on 13 RxP he will play 13 . . . P-B3 winning the pinned Knight. But he overlooks an obvious resource!

| 13 RxP! | . . . . |

See Diagram 166. Here Black can set an interesting trap by 13 . . . K-R1. In that case White should get rid of the pin on his Knight by playing 14 B-B4 threatening 15 N-N6ch! followed by 16 BxB winning the exchange.

DIAGRAM 166

Black thinks he can win a piece by . . . P-B3

But White might answer 13 . . . K-R1 with 14 NxPch? expecting 13 . . . RxN??; 14 R-K8ch (the back-rank mating idea), R-B1; 15 RxRch, BxR; 16 QxQ with a Queen for a Knight; or 14 . . . B-B1; 15 QxQ, RxQ; 16 RxB mate.

However, after 13 . . . K-R1; 14 NxPch? Black plays 14 . . . QxN!; 15 QxB, QxPch; 16 K-R1, Q-B8 mate(back-rank mate).

        13 . . . .   P-B3??

This is the point of the trap; but it is Black who succumbs, not White.

        14 Q-N3ch!   . . . .

The resource that Black overlooked. If now 14 . . . R-B2; 15 NxR, QxN; 16 R-K8ch (Black's Queen is pinned!), B-B1; 17 B-B4 and Black's Knight is lost, leaving him a Rook down.

        14 . . . .   K-R1

Overlooking the coming mate.

        15 N-N6ch!   Resigns

For if 15 . . . PxN; 16 R-R4 mate. An instructive game.

SICILIAN DEFENSE

National Intercollegiate Championship, 1929

F. REINFELD   N. GROSSMAN

White	Black
1 P-K4	P-QB4
2 N-KB3	N-QB3
3 P-Q4	PxP
4 NxP	N-B3
5 N-QB3	P-Q3
6 B-K2	P-QR3
7 O-O	Q-B2

This early development of the Queen should have been preceded by . . . P-K3, in order to prevent the maneuver which follows.

8 N-Q5   . . . .

Taking advantage of the opportunity to harry Black's Queen. The move involves a Pawn sacrifice. (See Diagram 167.)

DIAGRAM 167

White plans a promising Pawn sacrifice

8	KNxN
9 PxN	NxN
10 QxN	QxP?

11 B-QB4   Q-N3

After two time-wasting Queen moves, he needs an additional move to get the Queen back to safety. Black's extra Pawn is of little value in the face of White's considerable lead in development. It is not clear how Black is to play out his King's Bishop and then castle. As for White, his course is plain: just keep on developing, and attacking opportunities will come of themselves.

12 B-B4   Q-B3
13 Q-K3   . . . .

Naturally White has no intention of easing his opponent's difficulties by exchanging Queens. (See Diagram 168.)

DIAGRAM 168

White has a tremendous lead in development

It is difficult, if not impossible, for Black to develop his pieces properly. If 13 . . . QxP; 14 BxQP keeps up the pressure. If 13 . . . P-KN3; 14 KR-K1, P-R3 (not 14 . . . B-N2 because of 15 B-KN5); 15 Q-KN3, K-Q1 (to stop Bx QP); 16 B-Q2! followed by B-B3 with an overwhelming game.

13 . . . .   P-K4
14 PxP e.p.   . . . .

It is important to capture in passing, for the more open lines there are, the more telling is White's lead in development.

14	BxP
15 KR-K1	K-Q2
16 B-KN5	Q-B4
17 Q-N6!	. . . .

(See Diagram 169.) White leaves both of his Bishops under attack—perfectly permissible under the circumstances as he threatens 18 QxNPch with fatal results for Black.

DIAGRAM 169

Both White Bishops are under attack!

17	R-B1
18 BxBch	PxB
19 QR-B1!	. . . .

Threatening a quick mate. On 19 . . . QxB; 20 QxNPch is devastating.

| 19 . . . . | Q-N4 |

Another offer to exchange Queens, which White naturally declines.

| 20 Q-K3! | R-K1 |

If 20 . . . P-K4; 21 Q-R3ch and White mates in two more moves.

21 R-B3!   ....

Doubling Rooks on the open Queen's Bishop file will decide the issue at once.

21 ....   P-Q4

In order to answer 22 KR-QB1 with 22 . . . B-Q3 preventing 23 R-B7ch. (See Diagram 170.)

DIAGRAM 170

White must crush Black's last defensive hope

22 Q-K5!   ....

Threatening 23 R-B7 mate or 23 Q-B7 mate.

22 ....   Q-N3

If 22 . . . B-Q3; 23 QxNPch, B-K2; 24 BxB winning at once, as 24 . . . RxB loses the other Rook.

23 KR-QB1   Resigns

White threatens 24 R-B7ch followed by mate next move. If 23 . . . B-Q3; 24 QxNPch, B-K2; 25 BxB wins. An impressive example of incisive punishment of time-wasting Pawn-grabbing.

12. Chess Etiquette

"Touch—move"

MOST AFFAIRS IN LIFE PROCEED MORE PLEASANTLY AND smoothly when we show courtesy and consideration for others, and chess is no exception.

The most important rule of chess etiquette is expressed very simply: "Touch—move." In other words, if you touch a piece, you must move it. If you make a move, you must not retract it. These are good rules to abide by in all games; observing the rules will avoid friction and recrimination.

Here is what the official International Rules have to say on the subject:

"A move is complete

(a) In moving a man from one square to another, when the Player has quitted the man.

(b) In capturing, when the captured man has been removed from the board and the Player has quitted the man making the capture."

"The Player may adjust one or more of his men on their respective squares after giving previous notice of his intention to do so."

"If the Player touch

(a) One of his own men he must move it.

(b) One of his opponent's men he must take it."

Naturally the Rules assume that the moves in question are legal.

But there are other ways of annoying an opponent.

Donald MacMurray once described them with delightful humor in the first issue of CHESS REVIEW.* Here is what he wrote:

The Gentle Art of Annoying

"AS EVERYONE KNOWS, THE WORST THING THAT CAN HAPPEN to a chessplayer is to lose a game. Because this is so, it is evident that what the chess public needs is a method of winning easily without first mastering the difficult and unnecessary technique of making good moves.

"To begin with, you must realize clearly that your principal object is to disturb your opponent as much as possible in order to distract his attention from the game. Of the numerous ways of accomplishing this, the easiest and most common is talking.

"Talking to annoy may be done in several ways. You may, for example, talk *to your opponent*, either pointing out bad moves to him, or making any other misleading remark about the position. If your opponent so much as comes near to touching a piece it is always disconcerting to say sternly 'Touch—move.' If this involves you in an argument with him, so much the better for your chances of upsetting his train of thought.

"An example from actual experience will serve to demonstrate the practicability of this piece of advice. Several years ago, in the interscholastic championship tournament in New York, there arose an endgame position where White, who was on the defensive, had only one way of saving the game, to wit, by pushing a certain Pawn. He permitted his hand to hover over the Pawn, without touching it, whereupon

*Donald MacMurray was a very promising master who died at a tragically early age. The whole article is of course written tongue in cheek, but it points a moral for all of us!

Black cried gleefully, 'You touched it!' White denied the charge vigorously, and, when the referee finally decided the fight in his favor, triumphantly proceeded to move another piece, thus losing the game.

"You may also talk to the kibitzers, preferably discussing the previous game with them so heatedly that you draw your opponent into the argument, and so take his mind completely off whatever he was considering.

"If you like, you may talk *to yourself*. Every chess club boasts at least one genius of the talk-to-yourself school. Curiously enough, the favorite method of these experts is the recitation of nonsense rhymes. The eminent champion of the West has great success in declaiming passages from Lewis Carroll's *Hunting of the Snark;* while one of the most prominent American professionals has confided to me that about half of his yearly income is derived from the recitation, at critical points in his games, of *Mary Had a Little Lamb.*

"Another ready means of annoying which you have at your disposal is music. There are several different ways of employing music for this purpose. If you are a timid player, you may try humming, which is the most unobtrusive of the lot, and the least likely to call forth rebuke, but which, when raised to high pitch and accompanied by the gestures of a conductor, will throw your opponent entirely off his game.

"As your courage waxes, you will find a shrill, piercing whistle more effective than even the most artistic humming. The tune must be one far too difficult to be whistled correctly, so that it will sound at best like an undecided peanut-roaster.

"Finally, being carried away by the beauty of your noises, you may break into full song, accompanying yourself as before, with appropriate gestures, or else by tapping in time with your feet.

"If you do not happen to be musically inclined, you will still find a big field open to you in drumming and tapping, either with hands or feet. This is one of the best ways known to induce your opponent to make a hasty move, and is favored by nearly all of the masters who have no confidence in their singing voices.

"Other great resources which you possess are coughing, sneezing, and blowing your nose during the progress of the game. These are to be used freely, especially during the wintertime, both as a general distraction and to instill in your adversary the fear of germs.

"Similarly, when your opponent does not move quickly enough to suit you (and if you are a right-minded chessplayer, this should be nearly all the time), you should first heave a sigh, then yawn and look at your watch, and finally groan mournfully.

"A large class of nuisances not yet touched upon comprises those which aim at distracting the visual attention of the enemy. Of these, the one most highly sanctioned for your adoption is the system of blowing smoke rings across the board. This is useful, not only because it obscures the position, but also because it will surely get into your opponent's eyes or choke him, and thus put him completely at your mercy.

"Another annoyance of this type is adjusting pieces which you would like your opponent to take, or else pieces which are on the other side of the board from where your threat is.

"If you habitually rest your head on your hand, be certain to keep your elbow constantly on the edge of the board, shifting its position from time to time so as to be always concealing under it at least two or three important squares.

"As the evening wears on, you may resort to stretching, in doing which you should take care to fling at least one arm all the way across the board.

"Whenever you have what you think is a fairly good position, rock your chair back and forth on its hind legs, assuming meanwhile a complacent attitude, with your thumbs in your vest-pockets, as much as to say, 'Why do you not resign, you duffer?'

"There is only one more kind of disturbance worth mentioning. Although it is infrequent of occurrence, and, when it does happen, it is entirely accidental, it is as upsetting as anything else. It is making a strong move."